D1558439

CRAFTING TURQUOISE JEWELRY

Crafting Turquoise Jewelry

THE BASICS OF STYLE AND TECHNIQUE

BOB POWERS AND MARC BARASCH

Illustrated by Helen Zane Jensen

Stackpole Books

Published by
STACKPOLE BOOKS
Cameron and Kelker Streets
P.O. Box 1831
Harrisburg, Pa. 17105

Published simultaneously in Don Mills, Ontario, Canada
by Thomas Nelson & Sons, Ltd.

Color photography by Jim Gritz and George Holmes

Printed in the U.S.A.

Library of Congress Cataloging in Publication Data

Powers, Bob, 1942-
    Crafting turquoise jewelry.

    Includes index.
    1. Jewelry making—Amateurs' manuals.
2. Turquoise. I. Barasch, Marc, joint author.
TT212.P68   739.27   78-12277
ISBN 0-8117-1803-4

Contents

CHAPTER 1

On the Antiquity of Turquoise Jewelry

"History . . . bah!"

Unknown student in antiquity.

How long ago turquoise was first used as a jewel of adornment is completely lost—there is no way to tell at this late date when some ancient ancestor found a blue-green stone in some antediluvian time and fastened it a curious way to whatever he or she happened to be wearing. Turquoise was certainly in fairly widespread use in the First Dynasty of Egypt (the Egyptian word for beads was *sha-sha* and the symbol *sha* was the word for luck) probably an early reason why turquoise, alone among stones, has always had a *positive* mystical ability.

One of the first direct references to turquoise is in ancient Egyptian hieroglyphics in the word *mafkat.* Initially, scholars translated the word as malachite, an ore of copper, but now there seems to be little doubt that the reference was to the "blue gold"—turquoise. Why it was originally thought to refer to malachite is unclear—the word appears all over the rock carvings on the cliffs and mountains surrounding the turquoise mines in the Sinai Peninsula. Ancient papyrus records are even more exact: *mafkat* was diligently mined, mostly under Egyptian rule, from about the First to the Twentieth Dynasties. During this period, turquoise was a basis for scarabs, the Egyptian sacred beetle, and a treasured symbol of good luck.

The Bible has been combed for references to turquoise, but the results have been satisfactory only to some students—the stone is not immediately identifiable among the numerous stones which the Bible lists as sacred or used for personal adornment.

Much of the mystical antiquity of turquoise has been attributed to several incorrect translations or statements attributed to the wrong people. Aristotle, that one to whom so many like to refer in the hopes that it gives validity where none existed before, is supposed to have mentioned that turquoise prevented death by accident and was good for stings of scorpions (curing them, that is) and defense against reptiles. Actually, it was Ahmed Teifascite in the thirteenth century who said Aristotle said that (Aristotle lived from 384 to 322 B.C.). As with many other ancient references, the translation's meaning was in the eye of the beholder: Aristotle was talking about $\Sigma \acute{\alpha} \pi \phi \epsilon \iota \rho \sigma \delta$ (translated means "the stone that is blue and looks like this!") which is most often associated with the lapis-lazuli stone.

Theophrastus did a book on precious stones about A.D. 315 in which he discusses the properties of what is now known as odontolite—the first mention in history of *bone turquoise*, sometimes confused with the real stuff.

A five-volume monstrosity on the medicinal properties of various minerals and stones, written about A.D. 50, confused turquoise again with lapis-lazuli and mentions the bit about scorpion stings (immunity by wearing a stone). The Arabian authors of the thirteenth century who got plenty of their material from older works frequently confused lapis-lazuli with what later authorities began to call turquoise—this has led to a historical assumption (not too improbable) that the ancients thought turquoise was only a form of lapis and not a separate stone. If true, this neat little explanation could explain the nearly irreconcilable differences in early mentions of various stones which almost sound as if turquoise is being described.

The Roman author Pliny wrote EVERYTHING THE ANCIENT KNOWS ABOUT STONES (also known more respectfully as his book 37 of *Natural History*). In his various ramblings about precious stones, he talks about the material *callaina*, which has been accepted as being turquoise by most authorities. *Callaina*, Pliny remarks, is, ". . . pale green color. It is found in the countries that lie at the back of India, among the Phycari, namely, who inhabit Mount Caucasus, the Sacae, and the Dahae. It . . . is covered with holes and is full of extraneous matter . . . the finest of them lose their color by coming in contact with oil, ungents, or undiluted wine . . . some writers say that this stone is to be found in Arabia also, in the nest of the bird known as 'melancoryphus'.''

Well, enough of that. Turquoise jewelry in one form or another was apparently well known in the ancient and medieval world in more places than we once supposed. Galenus, writing in about A.D. 150 said the best turquoise stones came from the mines at Neisabur and were exported all over the known world. The Neisabur referred to is Nishapur, Persia (Iran). Alexander Trallianos in the sixth century mentioned turquoise as a cure for epilepsy. A century later, the Bishop of Seville mentions "Orientals" wearing turquoise stones in their ears. A hundred years later, turquoise is first talked about in Tibetan literature. Two kinds of turquoise are described in *The Four Tantras,* a Tibetan work based on a Sanskrit original, also in the eighth century.

In those days, it seems there were about a hundred years between takes: about the middle of the ninth century a book called *De Lapidus* clearly describes our illusive stone. "This stone is green, and the green color is like that of the sea. It changes its color according to the changes in the air . . . oil dulls its color." Over in Arabia, the Persians took up the thread of turquoise in literature. In 978, Ibn Haukal wrote about the mines and villages of Nishapur, and a travel writer named al-Beruni went on and on glowingly about the Persian mines for the blue-green stones which brought good luck.

About the thirteenth century a book called *Properties of Stones* first mentions the stone from "Turkey", the *turcois.* The French form of the word, *turquoise,* has been with us ever since. An Arab botanist at about the same time in a monumental research work mentions two kinds of turquoise supposedly male and female from the Nishapur mines, ja-led *sakhamy* and *fidjidjy,* of which the ancient *sakhamy* was the most prized and valuable.

Getting closer to modern times, Marco Polo in his masterful adventure nonfiction novel of travel wrote about the production of turquoise in Kerman Province of Persia and in Caindu, China (the present area of Sze-ch'uan, if it hasn't been renamed again). A very scientific discussion and dissection of turquoise occurs in an Arabian book on mineralogy, also about Marco Polo's time.

The Chinese *Cho keng lu,* a book first published about 1366, talks about trade in turquoise stones, mentions the Persian mines, and describes the mining of the stone in China. Turquoise crops up in Hindu literature sometime in the fifteenth century, and an Italian work about 1502 speaks of the "Vulgar Opinion" that turquoise was useful to horsemen in keeping the horse alert and preventing damage from falls off same animal.

With the discovery of America in 1492, and the conquest of Mexico by 1519, turquoise, or something very much like it, appears extensively in the writings of the Spanish explorers and religious figures. This was *Chalchihuitl*, a stone much loved by the Aztecs, which appears all over the literature of the conquest period and later is so confusingly described that some authorities think it was jade, some turquoise and some both. (For those who have leanings to the Von Dänikan school of thinking, it is worth remembering that turquoise was mentioned in ancient writings as being "exported all over the world" and it is true that in some fashion it seems to have appeared in old Mexico among the Aztecs as well as in the European and Asian parts of the world, without, at the time, any known commerce between them).

Meanwhile, back in Europe, Thomas Nicols in his *Arcula Gemmea* (about 1653, London printing), says turquoise, which he writes as *turchoys*, are often sold for "two hundred crowns or more" if they have no matrix. "The breadth," he says, "of this stone doth appoint the price. That which is the color of verdegrease, or like unto a serene skie, without any black veins, is excellent."

With the coming of printing, more efficient travel books from all over began to mention turquoise and the ancient mines at Nishapur, from which the majority of the world's turquoise supply came (it still does, it seems).

Despite the stone's antiquity and the use of it in jewelry from probably the earliest times, it is interesting to learn that as late as 1815, it was not regarded as a particularly precious stone in a London book on diamonds and other precious stones.

And what of our stone in the present? What brought the ancient blue good-luck mineral to our attention rather than any other? As late as 1937, the Encyclopedia Brittanica devoted only a few paragraphs to turquoise. The same edition gives page after page of information about jade and the section on diamonds is extensive.

It was the Southwestern Indian tribes of America who eventually made turquoise a sought-after stone, on its own in traditional and modern settings, and in the beautiful, crafted styles famous to the American tribes. Curiously, the use of silver with turquoise is comparatively recent; its use dates from about 1890. In Europe and Persia, turquoise is most often set with gold—the Persian turquoise usually looks better with gold.

How turquoise, mounted in silver, eventually seems to have become the exclusive province of the Indians of the Southwest goes back vaguely to the South American Andean culture. Turquoise appears in the Andean Cupisnique culture about 500 B.C. In the Valley of Mexico, turquoise mosaics have been found which date to about 650 B.C.

The first big flourish of the Mexican turquoise industry was in what is called the Post Classic Era about A.D. 900. In the same broad period, from about A.D. 100 to A.D. 900, turquoise is found all over the American Southwest, probably indicating trade routes and commerce between the Southwest and Mexico that were much more extensive than was previously thought. In the tenth and eleventh centuries, turquoise is increasingly found in the American Southwest, culminating in a find of 65,000 turquoise artifacts, fragments, and unworked pieces at the ancient site of Pueblo Bonito in Chaco Canyon, New Mexico. It is obvious from the archaelogical evidence that the old pueblo peoples of the Southwest were really *into* turquoise for adornment, mining, trade, the whole game of ancient commerce.

Prehistoric evidence of turquoise has been reported from California, Nevada, Arizona, and New Mexico (where much turquoise is found today). An ancient pit on Mount Chalchihuitl in the Cerillos mining district of New Mexico has debris from the main pit that cover 2½ acres which is about 100,000 tons of rock. Prehistoric mines near Manassa, Colorado, have pits fifty to sixty feet deep and 100 feet across by 150 feet long. There are 270 ancient mine workings in the eastern part of the county of San Bernardino, California.

Three major areas of ancient turquoise digs have been found in Arizona, and there are at least 38 localities in Nevada with prehistoric workings. One report claims the Indians "simply turned over whole hillsides in their search for the sky-blue gem."

This tradition of the blue stone was inherited by the modern tribes of Indians in the American Southwest. They incorporated it into their jewelry which later became world famous and in this century made the turquoise stone one of the most popular in this country. Most of the handmade Indian jewelry is produced by three tribes: the Navajo, Zuñi, and the Hopi. In Arizona, it is often called "turquoise jewelry", while in New Mexico it is simply Indian jewelry. There are also jewelry craftsmen in several of the Rio Grande Pueblos.

Silver and turquoise apparently only became associated together in the last century and in this country. The first Indian silversmiths were the Navajos who learned the silver work from the Mexicans to the south about

1850 to 1860. It wasn't until the 1940s that the current style of sterling silver sheets and wire entered the picture. Before then the Indians melted down silver slugs, coins, and anything else silver that happened to be around. Both the Mexican and U.S. governments outlawed the melting of coins fairly early, but this didn't bother the Indians much.

The earliest silver pieces were wrought (hammered) or cast in silver and set with anything that happened to be handy on the reservations: garnets, opals, petrified wood, etc. It is fortunate for us that all of the prehistoric turquoise mining had left plenty of turquoise about, both on the surface and in the old workings.

The jewelry of the various tribes varies considerably, but it has in common the use of turquoise along with some other stones (abalone, coral, sapphires, and others). The Zuñi people are skilled lapidaries and silversmiths known for their beautiful inlay work. They live in Zuñi, New Mexico, a town which probably once was the legendary city of Cibola. The Navajos do little stone-cutting (lapidary), but do overlay jewelry. The Hopi also do plain jewelry overlay, somewhat more complicated than the simple but massive style of the Navajos.

The Rio Grande peoples of the pueblos of Taos, Cochiti, Acoma, San Juan, and San Felipe also produce jewelry, although it is not such a dominant part of the tribal economy as with the Navajos, Zuñi, or Hopi. The Santo Domingos make a rolled shell and turquoise necklace called a *heishe*, and are regarded as the great retail distributors of the native Southwest.

Turquoise is the legendary jewel of the American Southwestern Indian. It comes from the earth, is the color of the sky and the varied blues of the great oceans. The Hopi have a legend of a gentle spirit associated with turquoise and shell (the Hard Beings Woman or the Woman of Hard Substances). There are Navajo legends about the birth of the Turquoise Goddess or the Changing Woman. According to the Navajos, the Changing Woman was born on a mountain top as a small turquoise image after Mother Earth and Father Sky had come together.

It is a strange stone of antiquity, a chance product of geological and elemental action. It is, like many things, an accident, but a beautiful one, like a super-nova burst or a hybrid rose. It is a thing full of history, legends, stories, and thoughts as old as the oldest records of mankind.

It has been told that as the Ant People were preparing to take their bundles of dry earth and grass seeds to the upper world, First Woman told them to take bits of the hard, blue stone of the sky so there would also be some hard rock in the new world. So when the Ant People went through the sky tunnel, they bit off pieces of the blue rock and carried them to the surface of the muddy island. And so it is that we can still find beautiful blue turquoise. [From a Zuñi Myth.]

Turquoise and Its Habitat

Through caves, and palaces of mottled ore,
Gold dome, and crystal wall, and turquoise floor.''

Keats *Endymion*

Figure 2–1.   A jeweler of Benares.

$CuAl_6 (PO_4)_4 (OH)_8 \cdot 4H_2O$. A hydrated basic phosphate of copper and aluminum. Triclinic-pinacoidal. Not very romantic, mysterious, or adventurous, but that's turquoise. Rough turquoise appears as a thin vein or seam, sometimes as a nodule. Although a pure crystal of turquoise is not an impossibility, it is extremely rare. It is a brittle stone, easily fractured and oddly resembling ivory in its consistency. It will scratch ordinary window glass, but quartz or a good knife blade will scratch turquoise. It is called an opaque gem (because of this, unlike other gem stones, it is not faceted for jewelry but used in a convex form called a *cabochon,* or in a baroque, or free form cut), but thin slices of the stone are semi-translucent.

Probably the most perfect color for turquoise is found where it is rather impossible to wear it or to set up a good jeweler's workshop—in the depths of the mine where it was found. Turquoise is well known for its ability to change color (a characteristic which is usually attributed to the gradual loss of water—spontaneous dehydration), and it does just that when it is exposed to air. In the mine, deep in the dark place where it was formed, one hundred feet or more below the surface of the earth, turquoise can be an ethereal indigo. Up out of the mine and into the light and air, the rough turquoise fades to a lighter (though still beautiful) robin's egg blue.

Turquoise is usually found in desert country, rarely far from an arid zone. Good places to look for it as a mineral are in the American southwestern desert, Persia, Egypt, parts of China, and arid regions of Australia. Thankfully for the costs of mining (and the costs of the processed stone) it is not found at great depths in the ground but as a general rule, within 125 feet or so of the surface. The general rule, however, is broken in New Jersey, where turquoise has been found at a depth of 1100 feet down an inclined shaft.

According to some authorities, the best turquoise is a pure sky blue with no matrix. Matrix is a word describing the presence of foreign material along with the turquoise. As is usual in cases of personal opinion, other authorities like turquoise with a matrix of quartz, yellow to reddish limonite, or metallic oxide vein matter. Along with turquoise blue, a stone may have varying elements of a splash, a line, a nodule, of yellow-red, black, gray, and even white—traces of other minerals.

The origin of turquoise? After poring through a few learned texts on the mineralogy of turquoise, there is a temptation to pay more attention to the old Hopi legend that turquoise is lizard guano, than to the scientific explanation. Briefly: turquoise is never a primary mineral (meaning it is not characteristic of or existing in a rock at the time of its formation), it is secondary, and apparently formed by surface waters percolating through altered rocks containing apatite (the source of phosphate), and copper minerals. It is worth mentioning that rock phosphates and ex-guano deposits have no definite chemical composition, apatite is often tricky in this regard, and so the Hopis were probably right all along: lizard guano. Turquoise, like Spiderman, seems to be everywhere; it occurs in both igneous and sedimentary rock.

TURQUOISE MINES

The most famous turquoise mines in the world are in Persia at a place called Nishapur, Khorasan, Iran (oil is not the only commodity the Shah of Iran controls). For about 800 years, the Persian mines have produced the majority of the world's turquoise, at first with mining techniques based on stone tools, then picks, crowbars, and lately, on modern mining methods. One of the openings of the mine is called "Isaac's Mine" and by tradition, was discovered by the Biblical Isaac, the father of Israel. This suggests that the mine workings were providing turquoise as long ago as 2000 B.C. There were seven mines working in the area in the fourteenth century, and the history is fairly clear from that point.

From these ancient Persian mines have come the gems for crown treasuries all over the world, but especially in the Middle East. The turquoise from the Nishapur mines is divided into three categories (which we would probably call good, better, and best): *Arabi*, which is a pale green color, sometimes spotted, and generally of fairly low quality, *Barkhaneh*, an intermediate quality stone divided into four subgrades, and top quality *Angushtari*, meaning "ring stones." *Angushtari* is usually sold by the piece and is not remotely cheap. The best color is a deep sky blue with deep indigo-blue (*talkh* or "bitter") and any greenish tinge killing the top price. The best of the best has the indefinable quality of "zat" which is to turquoise what "water" is to the diamond or luster to a pearl. The best ring stones are supposed to come from the Khaki diggings in the Abdurrezzagi mine.

Before you go hopping a plane to Iran to get the best Persian, remember that some of the world's best turquoise also comes from the

United States (although to be truthful, very little of it is as good as the best Persian) and it is also cheaper, considering the plane fare. Not to mention the hassles with the customs people on both sides of the trip and the fact that it is not likely that you will be able to buy any rough turquoise for export. The cutting of the rough Persian turquoise into cabochon and baroque stones is a thriving business for the people of the country and so no rough turquoise is allowed to be exported.

If the contemplation of the plane trip to the wilds of Iran seems like an adventure (actually it isn't difficult), you might try the mines of Russian Turkestan where there is a large deposit (according to one authority) on Mount Karamazar, 24 miles northeast of Khojend in the valley of Biriouza-Sai near the Samarkand-Ferghana boundary. Samarkand is lovely, the mine is remote. If your spirits are really up for exploration there are some turquoise mines south of the place Shur-ab, 5 verst from the ramification of the roads into the valley of Shur-ab, almost southward and a bit westward, in the volst L'ail'ak, district of Kokand, Province of Fergana, Russia.

If your preference is more toward the English-speaking world, there are turquoise mines at Lurg, near Benalla, Victoria, Australia; it is green-blue turquoise, with quartz and slate. There are also mines in New South Wales and Queensland. Most of the Australian turquoise seems to be of low grade.

There is some apple-green turquoise in Germany and a very porous turquoise (which won't polish well) near tin mines in the department of Creuse, France. There is little or no turquoise found in South America, so forget the trip to Bogota using Columbia as a base of turquoise operations.

A bit closer to home are the turquoise mines in the United States. Turquoise occurs in the following states: Arizona, New Mexico (the oldest mines), California, Colorado, Alabama, Texas, Virginia, New Jersey, and Nevada (the most mines). Mostly, it comes from Arizona, New Mexico, and Nevada.

The most famous Arizona mine is at Bisbee, a well-known ghost town, now turned tourist attraction, home of Brewery Gulch and the once published *Brewery Gulch Gazette* (the local equivalent to the much more notorious *Tombstone Epitaph*). Bisbee wasn't always a ghost town, but has frequently been a tourist attraction. Located at the foot of Mule Mountain, it was once a thriving community of mining families employed, for the most part, by the Phelps Dodge Corporation. The Bisbee Mine was the first large open pit copper mine in Arizona, begun in the early 1900s. In the upper layers of the giant pit, there was very fine turquoise, and as the hole descended into the earth, some of the most fascinating and beautiful turquoise ever seen was uncovered.

Turquoise at the Bisbee mine came in stringers up to two, sometimes three, inches wide, and in small nuggets in granite and quartzite. The material is often deep — small stringers of turquoise have been found at the 1,200 foot level of the Cole Shaft. The Bisbee deposits have very little chalky material; the stone is usually deep, intense blue, with a dark limonite-stained matrix. Bisbee, or "Bisbee blue" is harder than some turquoise and takes a good polish.

The Phelps Dodge Mine at Bisbee has closed down (although there are the usual daily rumors of it opening up again), but there is a concession to mine the old dumps for turquoise and collect the material from the mine. From 1970 to 1974, about 2,000 pounds of good quality turquoise have come from the mine workings.

Probably the second most famous turquoise deposit in Arizona is at Morenci, the largest open pit copper mine in the state. Turquoise was mined there by the Indians in prehistoric times. Morenci turquoise has the reputation for being one of the most beautiful examples of the stone found in Arizona. If you are a real wheeler-dealer, Morenci is the place to go; an extensive turquoise deposit was simply covered up by thousands of tons of waste rock some years ago and is still there, waiting to be recovered. Despite the increasing value of turquoise, it would be too big and expensive a project to try to recover this vast deposit of the stone at the present time.

The Morenci deposits (recovered by a firm in Gallup, New Mexico) consistently produce a top quality turquoise which has the characteristic most associated with Morenci turquoise: dark iron pyrite inclusions in the bright blue stone.

At Kingman, Arizona, is the Mineral Park Mine, once dug in prehistoric times, later mined by Arizona Indian Tribes, and producing by modern methods since about 1883. Another open pit copper mine, it has probably given up more turquoise than any other mine in Arizona. In 1973, Mineral Park produced over 23,000 pounds of green chalk, 54,000 pounds of blue, and more than 4,000 pounds of top grade, gem quality turquoise. The best stones are a clear blue with a relatively small amount of matrix, although some are a darker blue with hints of green color. The matrix is quite striking at times, often shot through with whitish pyrite (an arsenic-base), jet black (shiny chalcocite) and sometimes a clear prism of quartz.

Another brand of Arizona turquoise is "Pinto Valley" which comes from a mine originally opened in 1943 as the Castle Dome Mine. It is about five miles west of Miami, Arizona, and owned by the Cities Service Company. This mine, which produced molybdenum and copper during the Second World War, puts out about 9,000 pounds of turquoise each month. Along with a great quantity of poor quality, low-grade turquoise, the Pinto Valley mine has produced some good blue material.

Nevada has become the largest producer of turquoise over the last few decades, and it has the most diversified mines. Blue Gem, a beautiful turquoise brilliant blue, is often lumped under the generic name for the whole turquoise-producing area from which it comes, Battle Mountain. Battle Mountain Turquoise is well known for a lovely tan-brown matrix spread fairly evenly throughout the stone. The Blue Gem mine is another product of World War II. It was discovered about 1934, but was closed in 1941 when the experienced miners were called to the war effort operations. Blue Gem also produced some very fine blue-green and pure green stones.

Fox Turquoise, a generally medium grade stone, low in color, beauty, and quality, comes from near Crescent Valley, Nevada. Another prehistoric mine, it was officially "discovered" about 1912 and at one time produced about 2,000 pounds each month. The turquoise is greenish, with some blue. Despite the general lack of quality, Fox Turquoise has one redeeming worthwhile quality—it is hard. Because of the hardness, it is ideally suited for artificial coloring and tons of it were sent, at one time, to Idar-Oberstein, Germany, for dyeing. Even with its medium-grade, it makes a fine "manipulated" turquoise stone for jewelry making.

Lone Mountain Turquoise is, to many people, the most unusual and beautiful of all the types of turquoise mined and found. Long Mountain Turquoise is the "spider web" turquoise. Once named the Blue Jay Mining Lode, the deposit was mined for several years and then leased to another miner. It was the second look into the mine which produced what was to become a much-prized turquoise. At about 40 feet into the ground, Bert Kopenhaver ran across turquoise with a "spider web" matrix. At 84 feet, more was found. Lone Mountain Turquoise ranges from a clear blue to the spider web. Unlike some turquoise, it is known for keeping the same color. To make the mine even more distinctive, there is also the "fossil turquoise," named because it forms in the rock where parts of plant fossils have dissolved.

Again in Lander County, Nevada (which probably could be called the turquoise capital of the world), there is the Indian Mountain Mine on the south range of Bald Mountain. It produces about three pounds of turquoise a day in the warmer months. In winter, the mine is not worked, as it is buried under 10 to 12 feet of snow, 75 miles away from anything. The turquoise from the Indian Mountain Mine is hard to mine because it occurs in heavy black chert and schist (chert is a very hard glassy mineral, mostly silica; schist is another word for slate to some, and it is a crystalline rock). Dime-sized nuggets from the mine are very high grade.

Careyco Lake Mine in Nevada produces an "unpatterned" turquoise. It runs from light apple-green to a dark blue, is consistent in hardness, and rarely has any matrix or pattern. Near a ghost town called Tenabo in Nevada is the Stormy Mountain Mine, an extremely high quality turquoise producer. Stormy Mountain is very hard, dark blue flecked with black chert and schist matrix. Some other examples from the mine exhibit a sea-green, and some of the best grade stuff runs in a vein about one inch thick.

Two other well-known Nevada mines produce excellent and beautiful turquoise. Near Tonopah is the Royal Blue Mine which was discovered in 1902. The Royal Blue is one of the largest in Nevada and produces about 1,200 pounds each month with a fine matrix running through dark-sky-blue to pale, pale stones. The mine also produces a beautiful example of fire green turquoise, looking a little unlike turquoise as we imagine it. If there were Irish turquoise, this would come the closest to being what it should look like. The best from the Royal Blue Mine is in a limonite-stained rock in veinlets and seams with nodules which are sometimes over an inch in thickness.

Lander Blue, near Tenabo, Nevada has given us the best spiderweb known. It is not an extensive deposit, but a very rich pocket. While it was in operation, the Lander Blue produced only spider web, and the best spider web at that, in light to deep blue with a dead black contrasting matrix.

Out in the Rocky Mountains of Colorado, one of the most notorious of mining districts of all times produces another wealth—this time a limited production of rich green spiderwebbed turquoise. Cripple Creek is now showing turquoise that is almost as valuable, weight for weight, as the gold which once made this mining district the talk of every territory and many countries.

New Mexico has the oldest turquoise mines in the United States. Near Hachita, in the southern part of the state just north of the border with Mexico, are several mines which produce a very rich green and some soft pale blue; most of it is a matrix turquoise. Also in New Mexico is the Azure Mine in the Burro Mountains about ten miles west of the present city of Silver City, New Mexico. It is in this area that a pure turquoise nugget was once found—weighing 1500 carats.

Turquoise in New Mexico was once mined by a rather brutal and, for the stone's importance and value, tragic way. Indians and hunters built fires against rock walls and cracked off large masses by then throwing water on the wall. Unfortunately for turquoise as a gem-stone, this little game inevitably destroys the color. At Cerrillos, New Mexico, south and slightly east of Santa Fe, there are mines which have been worked for centuries.

Other deposits of turquoise have been located in Alabama in Clay County. According to some sources, the mines there have been re-discovered just southeast of the town of Pleasant Grove, near Birmingham. The deposits have never been of any great importance to the turquoise trade. There are some California turquoise deposits near Kearsarge from which, in 1949, a 7½ pound nodule was taken. There is a greenish turquoise in seams near the northern end of the Last Chance Mountains on the north edge of Death Valley.

Colorado deposits of pale blue to deep sky blue have been found at LaJara and there are deposits near Villa Grove, between Salida and Saguache. There is also a turquoise deposit about thirty miles from the old mining town of Leadville, Colorado in the Holy Cross Mining District.

Turquoise has also been reported in Texas, Kansas, and Nebraska, but the amounts and the quality have never been regarded as important. It has also been found deep in New Jersey and in Virginia in fairly small quantities.

For availability, turquoise has always been a feast or famine stone. The known deposits of commercial possibility or gem-quality (usually, but not always, the same thing), with a few exceptions are not particularly extensive. The inclines, shafts, and tunnels don't run on for miles with gleaming turquoise waiting for the picking as some people think. Some mines, it is true, produce good quality turquoise for years, but most of them are only productive for a few months or for a year or two. Often, many years have passed since a mine has been worked, or a claim dug. With the demand for turquoise still at a relatively high plateau, more and more new claims are tried and older mines are re-opened with new owners trying to get into the game.

Books on turquoise list pages and pages of mines and prospects which make it seem as if there are hundreds of turquoise mines producing today. This is not entirely true, and even deceptive. Many "mines" are only mineral *claims* filed by miners who suspect, from the surrounding formations, that turquoise might be present in the locale. These claims too often turn out to be a "dry hole" or, at best, contain a very low grade turquoise called "oiling" turquoise, which is used only for cheaper decoration.

Just in case you happen to be the kind who likes to do everything from scratch, either for personal satisfaction or plain desire to be different, it is *still* possible (though unlikely) to mine your own turquoise, cut it, and then put it into your own jewelry.

The same pull which brought those restless ones across the great wastelands and plains, mountains and rivers to the mining boom of the West is still there, though highly modified in these modern times. The opportunity to prospect on public lands, called national resource lands by the U.S. Department of the Interior Bureau of Land Management, is still with us. The first difference from the old days is that almost all the obvious and good mineral deposits have been already staked out and the chances are getting slim.

To go out and be a first class or at least enthusiastic prospector, you will need to drop by the local, and usually friendly, Bureau of Land Management Office and check the status records to be sure the land you are interested in exploring is in fact *public land* and also that it is open to mining.

The next step is to study geology. Turquoise occurs in areas with copper mineralization in a dry climate. Turquoise is, in simple terms, a copper mineral produced by a weathering process. In a dry climate, for example the desert southwest, the water table is low. As the surface moisture hits the land and drifts on down to the current water table, it leaches copper from the host rock. The copper from the mineralized host rock is carried downward and re-deposited in open spaces in the form of copper oxides. These oxides are usually blue and green (azurite and malachite), but they are sometimes, if you are lucky, turquoise—that precious stone for hand-made jewelry that all of this fuss is about.

If you find something that certainly looks like turquoise, get a sample (first making sure that the area you are in isn't already staked as a claim—usually in the form of a rock monument or location notice placed there), and take it to a mineralogist or a geologist.

The stone you have, if you are like most amateurs, is probably not turquoise, but something else of similar (but not popular or valuable) nature. If it turns out to be the real thing, you will want to stake a claim for your mine, something like the "I Found It! Lode." Filing a claim is about the same in most of the states, particularly in the West. You place a location notice to initially protect your mineral interests. Location notices are standard forms available in most office supply stores or at the local county recorder's office. At the point of first discovery, the location notice is placed on the claim in a monument, which in most states is a 4-foot-tall, 4-inch square post or a pile of rocks from the area.

When the claim is well and properly documented and located, a copy of the location notice must be taken to the county recorder to be filed in accordance with the requirements of the state in which you have been prospecting. You must also identify the claim in the location notice with reference to some survey marker or a permanent natural feature or out-standing landmark (e.g., twenty feet southwest of the lower northeast corner of the National Bank Building in downtown Dallas). This is a federal government requirement, mostly designed to protect your inter-ests. After the claim location has been filed, there is a period of time in which you have to establish the corner monuments (size) of your claim. Usually this is 60 to 90 days.

To establish corner monuments, you have to find out what the trend is in your claim, the direction or extent of the vein of turquoise. Since our beloved stone is normally in a seam, fracture, or vein, you generally have what is called a lode claim. As a rule, the maximum size for a lode claim is 300 feet on either side of the vein and 1500 feet along the line of the vein. A typical lode claim might be 600 by 1500 feet shaped like a paral-lelogram. Most states require that you mark the boundaries of each corner by a small cairn of rocks or a solid stake.

Now you are a turquoise miner—or better yet, almost a mine owner. Most states require that you do a certain specified amount of work on the claim in a time period. Some states only require that it be mapped or permanently identified with a local landmark. It is wise to check and see what the regulations are for the state you are prospecting in.

Once all this has been done, you are entitled to extract minerals, in this case turquoise, from the public lands. To hold onto that right, and keep away the claim jumpers (who still exist today, especially where valuable or even low-grade turquoise is concerned), you have to actively work the claim. Each year there must be one hundred dollars worth of work on the claim and an affidavit of the work must be filed with the county recorder's office.

There are a few cautions which should be observed: in developing a claim, there will be heavy equipment in most cases. The equipment is capable of doing considerable environmental damage and you should check into this before trying anything extensive. The BLM office has experts to tell you about environmental damage from mining a claim. Don't go into old mines or diggings alone—they're dangerous, may not be open to you anyway, and you might conceivably be shot at.

By the time you finish with all that you probably won't want to make turquoise jewelry, so you can file the claim information and plans for trips to Persia along with other hope chest mementoes and buy your stones, like most of us, from reputable dealers or from some of the mine owners who will do all the work for you.

CHAPTER 3

The Mysteries and Mystique of Turquoise

"We are no other than a moving row
Of Magic Shadow-shapes that come and go
Round with the Sun-illuminated Lantern held
In Midnight by the Master of the show."

Omar Khayyam

The number of things turquoise is supposed to do, or be good for, or bring about, is enormous. This is partly because all stones seem to have acquired a legend of deeds or misdeeds, depending on the kind, and partly because turquoise, being such an early example of a gem stone, had plenty of time to take on attributes given it by primitive people. This is not necessarily only true in ancient or medieval times—stones retain today some of the associations which they have "inherited" from former times. Worse yet, there are plenty of people to believe in the super-natural characteristics of stone.

One expert in turquoise wrote that "Mythology may be defined as the superstitions of the ancients; folklore as the superstitions of the ignorant today." Perhaps this is not a bad definition. However, turquoise has piled up quite a record of supernatural abilities and associations and it is worthwhile to know, especially if you are going to work with, wear, and purchase turquoise, what it might do for or against you.

The most noticeable part of a turquoise stone is the color—usually blue—and the ancients made a great deal of the associations of turquoise with other important things blue. Blue is, of course, the blue of the sky (and green turquoise is the green of water, tying two big images to-gether), but blue has also been associated in much more specific and spectacular fashions.

The Nile River, for example, is named from the Sanskrit word, "nila," which means blue. Blue was also the sacred color of the Druids (how this bit of information has been determined without any resident Druids available for comment is interesting, but not a part of this book). The Jews used blue for high pontifical robes, and the Egyptian god Amun was usually colored blue. To the Chinese, green or blue was symbolic of heaven and for the Hindus, the god Vishnu was associated with blue.

The business with blue (and therefore with turquoise) is not confined to the ancient world nor to the north of Africa or Persia. In old German folklore, lightning is always blue, in Mexico, blue seems to have been the color for almighty authority. In the American Southwest, the tradition of turquoise association with heaven and the sky has continued to the present time.

It is a stone that is soft and was easily worked by the ancient tools and procedures and so became an important gem long before some of the others which we have also come to know in the modern world. Because of the ease and facility of working, and the widespread availability, turquoise has picked up the beliefs of each of the peoples which used it.

According to an Egyptian tale, a magic chant over a lost turquoise jewel caused waters to part and the jewel was recovered sometime about 4700 B.C. An eleventh century manuscript from Persia recommends turquoise as being good for victory, fortune, curing diseases of the eye, beating Maalox for ulcers, and is useful for scorpion stings.

Best of all, turquoise is supposed to be a good barometer for smog. If it shines the air is pure, but if it dims, the air is full of bad stuff and you should go inside and crack an oxygen bottle. Actually, turquoise as a test for the purity of air was used as far as about the twelfth century. But if it worked then, it should still do so—turquoise hasn't changed.

Aristotle seemed to feel that turquoise would keep the wearer from being killed and he remarked that it was never seen on the hands of someone dead in battle. He went on, however, to mention that that held true for "the great," so that possibility might not work for those of us in this mid-twentieth century democracy.

The stone has been said to have all of the attributes of the various remedies advertised on television and, with inflation, is probably cheaper. Turquoise will: drive away pains resulting from evil influences, help a fortunate day to pass (if looked at early in the morning), bring victory, make other people like you, cure diseases of the head and heart, hernia, swellings, flatulence, dyspepsia, insanity, and ulcers. It will also, in combination with other ingredients: cure epilepsy, dispel fear, remove any chance of drowning (should be worn by all sailors), and if you wear it on the first day after a new moon and stand staring up into the sky toward the lunar surface, it will make sure you get rich.

Turquoise is also good for your love life. It has long been called a potent love charm and is supposed to be an infallible test for truth in love. If your love gives you a turquoise ring, it better not begin turning white—according to legend, that is a sign of lessening affection. Leah, for example, when she was chasing Shylock, gave him a turquoise ring to try and help extract a proposal of marriage. Even today, in Russia, a wedding ring is often set with turquoise pieces, for longevity of the marriage.

The stone which we are dealing with is amazing. It will tell time. There are two ways. Suspend it from a string in a glass and it will tell time on the hour by striking the sides of the glass. It will also vary in color with the hour of the day (presumably lightest just before dawn and darkest blue just before sunset?). It will both keep you from falling off horses and keep the horse from getting tired because you haven't fallen off and left him alone.

Astrology, not to be slighted in the old days, (or today, if the current popularity is any indication) also had a connection to turquoise. Or perhaps the link was the other way around. Early associations for the stone were with the planet Saturn (it has also been associated with Venus and Jupiter) and under the proper sign, it was regarded as being an extremely potent jewel. Also at one time it was best to wear it set in lead.

Turquoise has long been associated with the month of December, in which it is supposed to be most powerful, but it has also reigned as a birthstone for July and occasionally for June. It is good for some days of the week: on Friday, wear a turquoise stone in a copper setting.

It is not known completely whether turquoise has certain euphoric capabilities, but one thirteenth century writer remarked that it induced "hilarity." It also apparently had (or has) contraceptive qualities, since a fourteenth century author mentions that the power of the stone is such "that the man who owns it cannot engender and the woman cannot conceive." It is good for preventing divorce, since it is reported to have the power to take away all enmity and reconcile man and wife.

It is a strange stone, this blue lump which takes its color from the sky above and the waters below. One by one, the great qualities of the other gems have been diminished and trampled by the light of science and reason: bright red coral (if set in a good expensive setting) attracts robbers, not the reverse; sapphires won't put out fire, we're safer with a Good Housekeeping approved chemical extinguisher; the diamond doesn't take away fear, if it's obvious-looking, it gives fear; the emerald no longer corrects eyesight, now we wear glasses.

But turquoise has one property which has not been probed, pondered, laughed at or done away with: sometimes slowly, sometimes quickly, often for no apparent reason at all, the stone becomes pale, or turns spotted, or changes color, and true natural turquoise stones which do this are much more common than those whose color remains fixed and permanent.

CHAPTER 4

On the Art of Getting a Stone

"But how I caught it, found it, or came by it,
what stuff 'tis made of, where of it is born,
I am to learn."

William Shakespeare

Acquiring a turquoise stone can be easily compared to going out looking for a good deal in a used car. Like the old country folk song, "Sometimes you win, sometimes you lose, sometimes you just don't know. . . ." Turquoise is a tricky stone and even experts are sometimes confused. People who claim to immediately be able to identify a particular "mine" of turquoise are always a little questionable. The only perfect way to exactly tell the nature, mine of origin, and true value of a piece of turquoise is to have the material chemically analyzed.

There are notable exceptions: really top quality turquoise can usually be identified as coming from a particular mine because of its characteristics. For example, high grade #1 Bisbee turquoise is a beautiful deep, deep dark blue with a smoke-black matrix. Top stuff Morenci is quite a bit more of a pale blue with a fleck matrix of iron pyrite. There are other tell-tales for top quality stones. Yet one finds that top quality stones are very difficult to get, especially in the last few years, and the price has gone up and up. For most users and for general crafting in turquoise, finances limit the stones to the lower quality grades where it is nearly impossible to correctly identify the origins. Anyway, with anything but natural turquoise, it is impossible to tell the origin of a piece except by chemical analysis. And plenty of turquoise is "unnatural" these days.

If you want a good piece of jewelry, try and find as good a stone as can be afforded. There should be no reason, even economy, which would encourage you to use anything but "true" turquoise. However, in the interests of knowledgeable buying and potential embarassment, it should be known that there are turquoise substitutes on the market.

The first category of substitutes are those natural stones which are often substituted for turquoise either because of extremely low price or immediate and plentiful supply. Among the "natural" substitutes for our favorite stone are: lapis lazuli (a beautiful stone in some settings, but it isn't turquoise), variscite, chrysocolla, malachite, and azurite.

Stones further afield are dyed to resemble turquoise: howlite, agates (of various kinds), and the lowly and easily found forms of common quartz.

There is artificial turquoise, constructed from the very same materials and with nearly the same chemical properties as natural turquoise. This perhaps shouldn't be said, not being a "purist" sentiment, but some artificial turquoise is quite beautiful. The artificial stones are even injected with a suitable matrix and the material is molded to be a good ringer for the real stuff.

The worst form of turquoise hype is the plastic stone, dyed to be a nice artificial blue. When touched by something hot (needle, soldering iron, spoon, etc.) it melts. Plastic stones, by the nature of the construction process nearly all look uniform and of a uniform (artificial) color. They're not too difficult to spot and anyone who offers a top grade "Bisbee" for $10.00 for a big chunk is handling modified petroleum.

In addition to the obvious turquoise fakes that are offered in the market, there are four kinds of real turquoise that are, in one form or another, different from a pure, original, and highly prized "natural" stone.

Reconstituted turquoise is composed of real turquoise fragments mixed with various resins. When ground, the fragments are formed into new stones with the binding agent. This form of stone is much lower in shine and luster than natural turquoise and being composed of ground up fragments, it *does not have any matrix.*

There are several ways in which low grade turquoise is treated to improve the quality and appearance of the stone. Usually, the treatments are not permanent, and have varying degrees of success. DDT has even been used to treat turquoise, especially the softer grades (the amount used, however, is very tiny and probably not harmful to the wearer), as have several petroleum bases. Petroleum paraffin is used to fill in the pores in turquoise and bring out a green-blue color. It is injected under heat and pressure into the stone to improve the hardness as well.

Mineral oil or animal fats are sometimes used to treat low grade turquoise. The material is injected into the stone under pressure and low heat where it fills in the pores of the softer varieties of turquoise and brings out the color. Mineral oil treated turquoise has a noticeably glossy blue, slightly greasy color on close inspection. Unfortunately, this process is rarely successful for a long period of time; the stone slowly loses the fats and minerals through the pores, the color changes and the stone becomes chalky.

If the term "treated" turquoise comes up in dealing with a stone or piece, it is usually assumed one of the above processes has been used and that the material is essentially low grade.

Yet another form of altered turquoise is "stabilized" stones. Stabilization is used with turquoise which has a good natural color and matrix, but a high porosity. High porosity turquoise will absorb body oils and other materials it comes in contact with and change color. The stone may be a high quality piece, but its natural state doesn't make it a good gem to wear. The porosity problem is cured by injecting sodium silica gel or a clear, colorless polymer plastic into the pores. The pores are sealed, the stone is hardened and the original color is preserved. "Stabilized" turquoise has the intention of *saving* the stone—it is not necessarily an attempt to disguise low grade products. When finished, a stabilized turquoise stone is nearly impervious to air, oils, or most chemicals.

If the term "manipulated" turquoise comes up in dealing to get stones, don't worry. The ancient Persians held stones in their mouths to intensify the colors just before selling them—a form of manipulating turquoise. Generally, the word is used to give an overall description of the three forms of re-working "natural" stones: stabilized turquoise, treated turquoise, and the reconstituted stones.

If it sounds as if there is little chance of getting a first class top grade stone for your work, that's probably true. Of all the products of all the turquoise mines in the country, only about eleven percent is high grade gemstone. The remainder is rated on a fourteen point scale down to the lowest of the low—a porous completely colorless chalk-like substance. Treated and stabilized lower grade turquoise makes beautiful jewelry, it is nearly indistinguishable to the eye from natural stone, and it's vastly cheaper than top grade. In trying to get gemstone grade turquoise there is always the risk, especially at first, of being taken by the seller. Better to know a nice piece is lower grade and nicely priced than to lay out a good chunk of cash for what you thought was a fine gemstone quality turquoise piece only to find that it was a chemical nightmare.

It is important to remember that the stone we are dealing with is *not a diamond*. A diamond is nearly impervious to anything the earth or much else can throw at it—it will retain its inherent characteristics despite everything. A turquoise stone is delicate and precious in its beauty, easily destroyed by a little heat, (hot grease will ruin one); so brittle that a slight tap can often fracture one; and its color, an essential part of its price and beauty, is as easily changed as the seasons. Some turquoise will even change color just after mining—from exposure to the air and sunlight. This is not to imply that you shouldn't wear turquoise stones and enjoy them; that's what they're for. But care must be exercised in handling and wearing turquoise if it is to stay the way it was when you originally acquired it.

Assuming that what you have decided on is a "natural" stone and you want to look for one, there are four major factors by which a piece of natural turquoise is judged: color, matrix, density, and the size of the stone. And before going into the characteristics of a natural and probably expensive stone, remember: like plastic flowers, stabilized turquoise ("unnatural") has some advantages. Plastic flowers don't need water, stabilized turquoise doesn't fade. Stabilized turquoise is good for the same reason a poster is cheaper than an original oil painting and antiqued furniture looks a lot like antique furniture. Someone once pointed out that any car can be made as quiet as a Rolls Royce, as well painted, as mechanically powerful, and it can be made cheaper and more easily available. There is only one problem: it is *not* a Rolls Royce. So it can be with turquoise. Only a piece of natural true turquoise looks like what it is, and despite the disadvantages (ever try to get a Rolls repaired cheaply?), there is something about having it that can make it all worthwhile.

The color of a piece of natural turquoise was once one of the major factors in value. It is no longer the big determining factor according to some experts, but with all gem stones, things can become very subjective. Like art, there are plenty of opinions and lots of disagreement. The best test of a piece of turquoise is whether *you* like it, whether *you* will be comfortable wearing it, and whether five years down the road it will look as good to the eye as it does now. Please yourself, it's your jewelry, your budget, and your taste. If you like it, buy it.

The color characteristics of turquoise are related to the richness and intensity and depth of color more than shade (blue, blue-green, green, etc.). A stone can easily be light green but very *rich* (as opposed to pale and washed-out looking). It may also have a very intense, brilliant look (as opposed to dull, lifeless, and flat).

Some turquoise seems to have great depth—it seems to the viewer that he can see right into the interior of the stone. Other stones appear as if the color was brushed or painted on the surface. The latter stone is called "occlusive."

As far as the color of turquoise is concerned, there are some people who maintain that robin's egg blue is the only real and true turquoise color (and Siamese cats are the *only* true breed of cat, and Mercedes Benz is the only *true* car, etc.) while others believe that the color is up to the buyer. One survey, not a large one, taken some years ago indicated that more men preferred blue turquoise and more women preferred green turquoise. Back to one of the original ideas: if you like it, buy it.

Matrix is another determining factor in the evaluation of a piece of turquoise. It is probably one of the key ingredients in determining value and certainly the major determining factor in telling where the stone was mined. Matrix in a stone has an influence on price and quality in three ways: density, binding, and pattern.

The density of the matrix material is every bit as important as the density of the stone. A matrix which is porous and soft (called "chalky") will not polish easily, if at all, and presents difficulties in trying to shape a stone (it "undercuts," wears away faster, leaving the surface uneven). Hard matrix takes a good polish, shapes well when ground, and brings out detail, color and depth, in the surrounding turquoise stone.

The "binding" is related to the permanence of the matrix in the turquoise stone. Quartz matrix, for example, will often fly out in chunks during cutting (and sometimes during wearing), because it is not well bound to the turquoise. A tightly bonded matrix is one of the characteristics of a good quality turquoise gemstone—the border between the two types of material is smooth and clean and it stays in.

The "pattern" of matrix, although a subjective matter for the most part, is critical to the value of a stone. If the matrix in the turquoise is very large and/or highly off-center, a certain amount of visual appeal is lost. Thin, balanced matrix is the most prized and this is the reason that so-called "spiderweb" turquoise is probably the most expensive and certainly one of the most wanted specimens.

"Density" of a stone is related to, but not the same as hardness, although the terms are often interchanged. Hardness is a measure of the ability of the stone to withstand abrasion. Density, on the other hand, is the amount of rock per unit volume or mass. A high density stone takes and holds a good polish and unlike a more porous stone, it will resist the attacks of penetrants (grease, air, water, corrosives). A "natural" stone has little protection—that's one of the characteristics that make it a natural stone. To get one of good value, the good things which a manipulated turquoise stone might have must occur in nature and that's a much smaller mathematical probability. Also it increases the cost of the piece.

The last factor in value of a natural stone is the size. The bigger it is, the more it costs. This is usually true of most stones and it is certainly true of turquoise. And, sadly, a forty or fifty carat stone does not cost twice as much as a twenty or twenty-five carat stone. It can be four times as much. Nature only makes so many, so big.

So, how do you go about getting *your* stone? First, there are a number of mail-order houses which deal exclusively in gemstones (some only in turquoise) which can sell various grades and sizes of the stone. A list of some firms is in the back of the book. Other books dealing with turquoise have similar lists and so do magazines in the gem trade. And the yellow pages yield, in most major cities, a list of gem and stone dealers where turquoise can be purchased. Magazines, better yet, have advertisements, and from one issue of a current gem or lapidary magazine obtained at the library, you can get the names, addresses, and telephone numbers of dozens of companies dealing throughout the country. Ask any librarian for the current magazines on gem selling, lapidary, jewelrymaking, etc.

The problem with mail order is obvious—you are at the mercy of the dealer, sight unseen. Probably, the best bet is to visit the gem stores in the nearest metropolitan area and begin looking at what is available and at what price. Hold a piece, feel it, show it against your hand or on your wrist. Get an idea of the stone, what colors you like, the shapes you seem to care for and the type of matrix that give you that "extra something" that the others don't.

The turquoise will come in one of three forms most of the time: a cabochon (from the French, *en cabochon,* meaning "like a bald head"), baroque (free-form), or rough.

Cabochons come in some standard jewelry sizes, but actually a "cab" can be round, oval, rectangular, or square and almost any special shape can be cut and polished into the cabochon style. A table in the back of the book lists standard sizes for round and oval cabs.

Unfortunately, nearly all turquoise (if not all) in this country has an epoxy backing about the same thickness as the stone. In theory this is used to give the stone strength and make a stable mounting base and to make the existing supplies of turquoise go further. In practice, it means that you will be paying a per-carat price for epoxy which is unfair, but that's the way things are.

Viewed from above, a cabochon is usually round or oval in various sizes. Viewed from the side, cabs are either low cabochon (used most often for turquoise because the low profile exposes less stone surface to breaking and the elements), or high cabachon. Turquoise is rarely made in the high cab because of its porosity and softness. Sometimes a "normal" cab is offered, and that is simply a curve somewhere between a low cab and a high one.

Turquoise can also come in a baroque cut, that is a free-form cut of whatever type is available or someone has made. And it can come in rough form from which a baroque or cab can be ground and polished. Persian turquoise is not available in rough cut. The Iranian government will not permit its export because the cutting and polishing to cab and other shapes is a good employment for a thriving industry. Persian turquoise is also not epoxy backed as is most U.S. turquoise, so a better value is possible (more stone and not epoxy for the money).

In most instances, the average craftsperson who is interested in making some jewelry for personal wear will buy a ready cut and polished cabochon of a standard shape and medium quality from a local or mail order firm. For those who want to go the whole way and make a stone from a rough chunk of turquoise, or several stones, the chapter on making a cabochon which follows will be essential.

CHAPTER 5

Roughing Out a Stone

"Work. There is nothing else."

Albert Einstein

The best way to get on with the crafting and creating of jewelry is to purchase a suitable stone from a local or national dealer. There are still those people who like to do projects from scratch, however, and if you have acquired a chunk of rough turquoise from one mine or the other, it is time to see what can be done with it to get it ready for the jewelry bench.

Turquoise is an opaque stone and so is usually cut into the form of a cabochon, a shape with a flat bottom and a rounded top. There are,

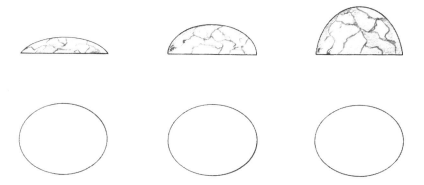

Figure 5–1. Side and bottom views of low, regular, and high cabochons.

although without much in the way of definitive parameters, three types of cabachons: low, regular, and high (Figure 5-1). Since turquoise is a soft stone and easily chipped and soiled, it is usually cut as a low cabachon to keep it surrounded by the setting and out of the way of things. A high cabachon turquoise, while probably beautiful, is a high risk item.

Most stones need to be sliced into slabs before they can be made into cabachon shapes, but few jewelry makers and amateur cutters own a slab saw. Although not horribly expensive, a slab saw is basically unnecessary since pre-slabbed materials are usually available. If not, a trip to a local lapidary shop with your prize hunk of raw turquoise will usually result in several slabs cut to your specifications which can be made into good cabachons.

Once you have a slab of turquoise about $3/16$ to $3/8$ inch thick, you can mark out the outlines of your cabachon on the surface. Most hobby shops and rockhound shops have plastic templates which make it easy to mark out an appropriate cabachon. Once you have the size of cab you want picked out on the template, place the template on the slab of turquoise and mark the outlines of the cab with an aluminium pencil (sharpened knitting needles work very well as an aluminium pencil).

Be sure to mark the outline heavily, tracing the cabachon lines several times on the rough. Once the outline is traced, it is time to grind away the excess material outside the cabachon shape (an oval is the easiest to cut). If your friendly local lapidary shop owner has a trim saw, he or she can easily and cheaply cut the excess turquoise away from the cab shape you've chosen. If a trim saw is not available, and you like to do things yourself, the turquoise can be ground off to leave a very rough cabachon shape. Luckily, turquoise is quite soft.

For grinding, silicon carbide wheels are used for most gem cutting. The soft bonded wheels are the easiest to use, but they are also the most expensive and they wear rapidly. The medium grades of wheels are the best compromise between economy and ease of use. Most wheels are available in several grit sizes: #100 or 120 is best for rough cutting and grinding and #220 is best for fine grinding.

No grinding wheel should *ever* be used faster than the speed recommended on its rim or label—the maximum safe speed for most wheels is usually about 6,000 RPM. If it won't cut, use patience, not more speed!

For most work, running an 8-inch wheel at 3200 to 3500 RPM is best. Slow speeds are all right, but they cut slow and the grinding wheels will develop unevenness and bumps.

For your motor, you need a used 1725 RPM ordinary electric motor, a four-inch pulley on the motor shaft (pulleys can be purchased from most hardware stores as can rubber belts to drive them) and a 2-inch pulley on the shaft that will turn the wheels at about the required speed. You *can* put a wheel directly on the electric motor, but the speed will be only 1750 and slow-cutting. The better arrangement is an arbor with two housings holding the grinding wheel and two pulleys to increase the wheel speed. The cost of such an arrangement is not large relative to the fun you can have with the rig.

When you first fit a new grinding wheel, stand back and turn it on, letting it run for about five minutes. It is not unheard of that a new grinding wheel will have some flaw which will cause it to come apart—at 1750 RPM or so it can make a terrible racket, not to mention the holes in the wall.

Turquoise, it must be remembered, is not only soft, but porous. The grinding lubricant *must be water*. The stone will absorb any oils and turn color.

Any grinding wheel arrangement should have a guard to keep out stray flecks of stone. With water as a lubricating medium (and quite a bit of water is needed) a splash guard/stone guard is a must—otherwise you may wind up cut, pockmarked, blind, and drenched, probably in nearly that order.

The "water connection" can be made in several ways: a large pail or pan which, by means of a small hose, lets water drip down onto the grinding wheel just ahead of the place where you are grinding. A transfusion bottle with hose and stand (if available) makes a very nice drip "oiler" for the grinding operation and it can be stood next to the grinding area, but out of the way except for the rubber tube. A catch pan or pail is also necessary for the water which drips toward the floor in the grinding.

Now that this messy sounding apparatus is constructed and ready (and it *is* messy), the rough cabachon which you have previously marked out is presented to the grinding wheel in the first step toward a piece of hand-crafted jewelry.

The side which you have marked out will be the "bottom" of the cabachon. A slow speed will give you much better control over the project, so if you have fitted a grinding wheel straight to the electric motor, instead of constructing a separate arbor with pulleys, it will go very slowly and you will have plenty of control.

The cutting should be done on a level just below an imaginary line drawn through the center of the shaft on which the grinding wheel is mounted horizontally. Beware of fingers and knuckles against grinding stones—they cut skin easier than they cut even soft turquoise. Above all, wear old clothes, or better, a rubber apron.

Begin by moving the rough stone back and forth over the entire surface of the cutting wheel, staying twice as long near each outer edge of the wheel as in the center (centers of grinding wheels soon develop a groove if you're not careful). Hold the slice of turquoise being cut so that the material which is ground away is at a ninety degree angle to the surface you've marked with the aluminium pencils. The idea is to wind up with an oval which has an upper surface like the marked outline.

The next step in cutting your cabachon is to grind a small bevel on the edge of the rough, partially cutting away the aluminium outline at a forty-five degree angle to the flat bottom of the stone. On a stone of about 20 by 30 mm, the first bevel should be about 1 mm wide. Be careful since it is easy to overcut, even at relatively slow speeds. This bevel has several purposes: it makes the stone easier to pick up from flat surfaces, especially if there is any liquid around it (suction, like trying to lift a flat plate up from a wet surface); second, it finishes off the edge of the bottom of the stone, making it sit flatter in a tight setting. A properly beveled stone is also much less likely to chip when it is being fitted, and as the top of the stone is being ground to form.

On the "top" of the stone, we will grind several bevels which will ultimately leave little to be ground down to make the rough turquoise piece become a good looking cabachon. First, however, the stone must be mounted for further work—it is probably, unless a relatively large stone, a little too small to work by hand without losing too much skin or parts of a finger or hand.

CHAPTER 6

Dopping the Stone

"Where shall we land you, sweet?"

Swinburne

From now on, the shape that the finished cabachon will take is entirely up to the care you exercise in the making of it. There is no magic formula which will show how to come to a good curve or a finely finished surface. What you do, you will see in the resulting surface.

Dopping is a term for putting a partly ground stone on the end of a stick with sealing wax or something similar. The stick then becomes a "dop stick." Dopping is usually done just after the profile has been ground, but before the top is worked. Dop sticks are easily made from 4 to 5 inch lengths of ordinary hardwood dowling available in hardware stores or most any lumber yard. The sizes available range in width, but for our purposes, dowels of about ⅛ to ¾ inches are about right. For stones of small to medium size, a ½-inch dop stick is a good size.

Dopping wax, for fixing the stone to the dop stick, can actually be made from ingredients, but it is not worth the effort; the wax is available in any store where the usual run of lapidary supplies is sold. The wax comes in sticks, the end of which should be heated and then a quantity transferred to the dop stick. An alcohol lamp is recommended for heating the wax, but it isn't necessary.

The dopping wax will make a really good seal to a stone only if the wax and the stone are at nearly the same temperature. One method is to heat the stone on a small piece of metal plate until a drop of wax dropped on the hot metal will melt. This means that the stone and the wax are about the same temperature. It is also possible to heat the stone by passing it through a flame with tweezers. The latter is not recommended because most stones are heat sensitive and some peculiar results can happen when they are heated in this way.

When the wax and the stone are the same temperature, press the stone onto the dop stick (be sure the dop stick is pressed onto the *back* of the stone) and shape the wax mass into a cone-shape with your fingers (be sure to wet your fingers before this operation, since wax will melt at a somewhat higher temperature than skin will blister).

With the soon-to-be cabachon fixed to the dop stick by wax, the next steps in the cabachon making can be begun. The stone is held sideways to the grinding wheel, and a twenty-five to thirty-five degree bevel is

Figure 6–1.   Start grinding the cabachon at an angle of twenty-five to thirty-five degrees; cut increasingly steep bevels.

ground all the way around the stone. Grind a little at a time, constantly revolving the stone. Once this bevel is well ground around the stone, cut a second one at a greater angle (see Figure 5-2). If it is a big stone, or you want to make a particularly high cabachon, several more bevels will have to be ground. The stone must be constantly inspected for symmetry of the bevels. Patience is more important in this operation than speed, especially with your first stone. Figures 6-2 and 6-3 show how the dop stick and stone are moved to make the bevels.

When all the bevels have been cut into the stone and you are satisfied with the symmetry of the work, the corners of the bevels are ground off, leaving a stone which is roughly the shape which you wanted (Figure 6-4).

With the bevels ground and the bevel corners smoothed off, the stone should be evenly curving in every direction, although roughly ground.

If the edge becomes too sharp causing the stone's outline in aluminium pencil to be lost, take the stone off the dop stick and cut it down to a smaller size. If the stone pops off the dop while you are grinding, the

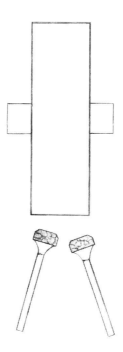

Figure 6–2. Alternate the sides being ground by approaching the wheel from these two directions. Grind a little at a time and inspect the symmetry of the stone often.

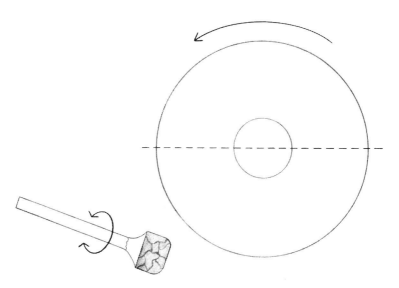

Figure 6–3. Twist the dop stick to even the bevels and prevent gouges.

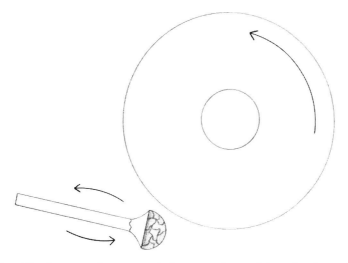

Figure 6–4. The last step is to round the stone by rocking the dop stick around an imaginary pivot.

wax was not hot enough or the stone and the wax were too dissimilar in temperature. If the former happens, it is also possible that the stone was oily.

Common beginners' mistakes are shown in Figures 6-5 and 6-6: uneven curve, a stone cut too steeply, a stone cut with too sharp an angle, and a clumsy curve. Last, and sometimes useable, is a stone which overhangs (for the cover-over-your-mistakes crowd).

Figure 6–5. The left-hand stone is correct. The second suffers from the common beginner's mistake of an uneven curve, the third has been cut too steeply and the fourth at too sharp an angle.

Figure 6–6. Correct stone, clumsy curve, and overhanging stone.

If all has gone well with the grinding on the stone, switch to a finer grit grinding wheel. If you have only purchased one grinding wheel (a coarse grit), then finish the same motions carefully with a very light pressure. This will approximate the grinding by a finer wheel, but it is not as good.

If the fine grinding wheel has done its work properly and you have been careful, the curve of the cabachon has now been fixed. The sanding and polishing operations do not usually alter the curve (they don't cut much material) and all that is now necessary is to get the stone into the final form for mounting in a piece of jewelry.

Sanding can be either wet or dry, depending on your preference. Various grits of sanding material come in disks which can be mounted onto the electric motor.

There is one important word about sanding which should be emphasized and the same thing goes double or triple for the polishing operation. DO NOT ATTEMPT TO REMOVE MATERIAL WITH A FINE GRIT WHEN THE DAMAGE HAS BEEN DONE WITH A COARSE GRIT. It won't work, is time consuming, and in the case of polishing, is nearly impossible because the cutting action of the polishing compounds is so slight.

If the fine grinding has been done with a good fine wheel (#220, or better, 320), then proceed to "sanding" grade disks of progressively finer grades. Be careful of heating the stone (test it against your palm) during sanding—in addition to getting a "burn" on the stone, excessive heat can melt the dopping wax and the stone will be airborne.

When the cabachon is smooth all over with the various grades of fine sanding used, wash everything thoroughly; stone, dop stick, and your hands (an old toothbrush is handy to get the grit out of small places in the wax). If you are satisfied that all the grit from grinding and sanding is gone from the stone and dop stick, you may proceed with the final stage of finishing a cabachon, the polishing.

Fine sanding should have left a stone which appears almost polished. If it is extremely rough looking and the surface is coarse and dull, you haven't done a good job of sanding. Polishing is usually done on disks of felt or leather with a compound: tin oxide, cerium oxide, or tripoli. Tripoli is the microscopic silica skeleton of long-extinct miniscule sea animals and is used normally for an intermediate grade polish.

If the sanding has been well done, a few minutes of polishing with one of the compounds will bring the stone up to a finished looking condition. The best test of the polish is under a magnifying glass for scratches and under a fluorescent lamp for surface curve. The best polished and cut stones will reflect light in a curve, like the stone on the left in Figure 6-7. If your stone reflects light as the stone on the right, then it will have to be recut.

Figure 6–7.   The test of a well-cut and polished stone. It should reflect light in an even curve. If it is like the stone on the right, it will have to be recut.

When the process has been completely finished (sometimes it takes longer to read about it than it does to do it), the stone is removed from the dop stick, and heat or cold will work. Heating the stick and the stone over a flame will get your gem in your hand much faster—putting them in the refrigerator or freezer will also work. To remove the last of the dop wax, the stone can be put in a small jar of alcohol.

If you want to make the back of the cabacon ground flat, as opposed to the surface left over from a slab or trim saw, it can be placed bottom down on a flat piece of glass (about 6 by 6 inches will do) and slowly moved around the glass with grinding compound between the bottom of the stone and the surface of the glass plate. This will result in a nearly completely flat surface with a good finish.

Whether you have chosen to try and mine a chunk of turquoise, saw cut, trim, and grind it into a rough cabachon, then sand and polish it into a beautiful gem, or you have chosen the easier method of buying a medium grade calibrated stone from a commercial source (or a baroque cut stone), you now have the first ingredient in a well made piece of crafted jewelry. Now it is time to learn about jewelry making and the ways in which this stone, whether sky blue or green or slashed with a dark matrix, can be put into an artistic background from which to glow, gleam, and delight the wearer and the beholder.

CHAPTER 7

Crafting Turquoise Jewelry

"The true artist, capable, practicing, skillful,
Maintains a dialogue with his heart, meets things with his mind . . .
The true artist draws out all from his heart;
Works with delight; makes things with calm, with sagacity . . ."
16th century Aztec goldsmith to Spanish conquistador

Turquoise and jewelry making have shared a common history ever since men first laid eyes on the stone. The desire to set that impossible blue color into an ornament, to adorn oneself with a piece of the sky, has proved an irresistible lure ever since early Neolithic times. Whether just an unpolished nugget strung on a thong or a piece of gem grade Persian surrounded by diamonds, turquoise jewelry has always been a way to touch and be touched by the elemental beauty of the world.

Indian jewelry, which has done so much to spark an interest in the craft, is only the most recent chapter in mankind's long epic romance with the blue gem. A well-heeled Egyptian pharoah would no more have considered stepping out his door without his inlaid turquoise ornaments than today's average movie star. Such was its significance among the ancient Aztecs that the wearing of the turquoise nose plug was a privilege permitted the Emperor alone; anyone caught displaying a different opinion was summarily executed.

Although lately more heads have been turned than lost over it, turquoise jewelry still provides a certain edge of excitement. It is a fillip of visual exuberance in the midst of our daily routine, a portable celebration which requires no other occasion than the fact of being alive. The soft radiance of blue against silver represents the valuing of beauty over

Figure 7–1.   If it all goes well, the next step is to put the stone in an appropriate setting.

monetary worth, of inner quality over outer appearance, that is rapidly becoming the spirit of an age.

As the popularity of turquoise jewelry has grown, so have the ranks of amateur craftsmen. With so much Indian work fallen prey to assembly-line production methods or outright cheap imitation, turquoise fanciers by the thousands are discovering the pleasure that can come from expressing their own ideas in silverwork.

ATTITUDES

"Teach us to care and not to care,
Teach us to sit still."

T.S. Eliot, *Ash Wednesday*

There is something immensely satisfying about sitting at a workbench and watching a complete work take shape. It is a form of communion with oneself, that same private moment of self-awareness we experience when, putting a shell to our ear, we hear the sea humming through the estuaries of our own bodies. Without even noticing, the craftsman enters a separate reality where the "big" and "important" things of the world recede against the horizon, suddenly made insignificant by a piece of metal several inches square.

However, make no mistake about it—jewelry work has its share of frustrations. Most beginners are woefully unaccustomed to the small movements of hand and eye which will later become second nature. A sense of humor is absolutely necessary in the process of getting the hang of a new technique. There are those times you make the most meticulous of preparations, only to watch everything go wrong for no logical reason at all. Worse, everything is done completely wrong and somehow you wind up with a textbook-perfect piece. You may wonder, as did the jewelers of old, if you've just fallen out of favor with one of the craft's patron deities.

The gods' good graces aside, the most important thing you will need is the proper attitude. A piece of jewelry proceeds to completion at its own pace, through progressive steps and gradual refinements. If you are in a hurry to see results, you will inevitably make mistakes. On the other hand, if you approach each step as an end in itself, the final work will emerge like a butterfly from a chrysalis, so full of its own being that you will find it hard to remember ever making it. However, as the old saying goes, "He who makes no mistakes makes nothing," and learns very little. Mistakes are a process of discovery; you will often learn more about the properties of the tools and materials from a single error than from all the times you do the same thing flawlessly.

Above all, it is good to remember that making a piece of jewelry is essentially play, a freeing of the aesthetic sensibilities under the influence of what Aldous Huxley once called "the natural magic of glinting metal and self-luminous stone." It is a realm unto itself, where all things are seemingly possible because none of them is really necessary. To enter it is to pass through the gates of the self.

TECHNIQUES

The methods of making simple jewelry have come through centuries of rapid technological progress surprisingly unchanged. The techniques we will be treating date back thousands of years, to the times of the ancient Sumerians, and are among the oldest and at the same time the most up-to-date in the modern jeweler's repertoire.

Generally referred to as "flat construction," the methods may be regarded as a "model airplane" approach. According to this technique, which has long been a favorite of native American craftsmen, the individual elements of the design are first sawed out with a jeweler's saw, then "glued" together using silver solder.

This method has several advantages. It is an easy way for a beginner to get accurate and exciting results from the start. Techniques like casting or forging, on the other hand, can take years before they yield much beyond the blobby or bent-up looking work that is too often passed off as "modern jewelry." In addition, construction techniques are inexpensive, requiring only a minimal outlay for tools and materials. At the same time, they provide the groundwork for an understanding of the craft as a whole. Using these methods, the beginner will, with a little care and patience, find that he is capable of producing jewelry of surprising beauty and complexity.

Techniques often vary wildly from craftsman to craftsman. If jewelers were more social animals than they tend to be, they would long ago have established nation states based on different solutions to identical problems. Although we have included some special "trade secrets" in the book in cases where they might prove helpful, for the most part the simplest and most unambiguous techniques are the ones that are recommended.

Theory has been presented only where it is applicable to the task at hand. There is no need to have a thorough knowledge of metallurgy in order to make simple jewelry. At the same time, as the great Renaissance jeweler Benvenuto Cellini once remarked, "Technical skill serves you up to a certain point; but, in some accident for instance, you need the deeper knowledge of the principles of the art." Since errors often require improvised solutions, a minimal understanding of how the different processes work will prove invaluable in helping you pick up the pieces and go on.

TOOLS

Man, anthropologists tell us, officially emerged as a species apart as soon as he learned to make tools. Interestingly, according to evidence gathered from the earliest sites, no sooner had he pulled off this evolutionary coup than he set about using his new-found talents to make, of all things, jewelry. Admittedly, the work wasn't much to look at: a few pieces of shell with holes punched in them, the remains of a bone necklace, a handful of roughly-hewn beads. Nonetheless, it was the start of the great jewelrymaking tradition which basically states "Make the most of what you have . . . and improvise the rest."

Constructed jewelry requires relatively few tools, all of which can be easily obtained from the hobby shop, hardware store, or in some cases the bottom of the "junk drawer" in the kitchen.

The most important thing to learn is the proper use of each tool. Using, for example, a fine needle file when the job calls for coarse scraping makes about as much sense as trying to barbecue an eleven ounce steak by flicking your Bic.

On the other end of the scale, it is not necessary to destroy your budget by buying expensive, specialized tools. Some of the greatest jewelry ever produced, and some which is greatly admired today, has been made with tools which by some standards would be hardly worth purchasing. Jewelry, like good photography, is more often produced by the eye and hand of the artist, rather than the name brand or the expense of the technical equipment.

MATERIALS

Turquoise and silver are ideal materials for the beginning craftsperson. Turquoise, besides being readily available in either natural or treated form, is one of the few stones that looks even more appealing in silver than in gold. Rather than requiring complicated settings, it is best mounted in a surrounding band or bezel of fine silver which sets it off handsomely as well. Since it is a relatively soft stone, it should not be worn when you are doing any sort of prolonged manual labor (like making turquoise jewelry!). Try to keep it free of oils or grease, as these will tend to make a blue piece take on a progressively greener cast. By the same token, do not, as is sometimes recommended, treat a stone with mineral oil to deepen the color. Although this has been widely practiced among dealers to "bring up" a lighter stone, the color change is not stable and in the long run the oil will make it duller than it was in the first place.

Silver is both a relatively inexpensive and easy-to-work-with material. One of nature's "noble metals," second only to gold in its malleability (ability to be shaped) and ductility (ability to be drawn into wire), it has been used in jewelry making ever since the craft began. The Aztecs, believing it to be the "tears of the moon," worshipped it as a divine substance. It is still used as a ritual mirror in certain oriental religious ceremonies (as well as in ceremonies of international high finance!). The most commonly used form of the metal is sterling silver, a term which derives from the medieval name for the Germans (Easterlings) who once refined England's coinage. It consists of "fine" (pure) silver to which a small percentage of copper has been added. It comes from the manufacturer in a wide variety of different forms—flat sheet, round, half-round, triangular, or square wire hollow tubing—all measured in standardized gauges (see Measurements, Weights, and Solutions).

The copper in sterling silver will cause it to tarnish, or "oxidize" in time. However, jewelry should not, as is sometimes done with copper and brass articles, be coated with nail lacquer or similar agents. This not only gives the work a cheap, artificial luster, but also prevents the metal from acquiring a natural patina. Silver will tarnish at a different rate on different individuals, but this is not, like Dorian Gray's portrait or mood rings, some portent of the inner being but merely a reaction to a particular body chemistry. If, for any reason, a piece gets too dark, it only requires a quick polish to shine it up to its original brilliance.

PROJECTS

Each project has been selected in order to acquaint the craftsperson with yet another of the virtually limitless possibilities of simple design and construction. They have their roots in a wide variety of design traditions, ranging from ancient Mesoamerican to modern Scandinavian. All have been specially adapted to fall within the budget and range of skills of the novice. Although they have been created especially for turquoise and silver, many of them will lend themselves to treatment in other materials, such as brass and tigereye, if for some reason nothing else is available.

Although the projects will be of interest to anyone who has ever sought a broader theoretical understanding of how jewelry is made, they were really devised to be put to more practical use. They are presented in the hope that even those who have never considered the craft might be tempted to take tool in hand and give it a try.

This book is a manual, not a compendium or a textbook of theory. It has been designed to be used. Although there is no substitute for a live demonstration of jewelrymaking, the way has been pointed out as simply and clearly as possible.

As the great Cellini put it in his sixteenth-century treatise on gold-smithing, "Really, it's quite impossible to tell it properly in writing; I could explain it all right enough by word of mouth, or better still show you how it's done—still, come along—we'll try and go on as we started."

CHAPTER 8

Design and Design Transfer

"I feel a strong kinship to stones. . . . I feel the stone and think, not to conquer it, but to help it express itself."

Charles Loloma, Hopi Indian silversmith

Turquoise comes in every conceivable size, shape, and color. Sea green or sky-blue, baroque or round, finished cab or rough nugget, each piece is an individual, pulsing with a life and personality all its own.

Designing an appropriate setting, especially for an irregularly shaped stone, is a little like meeting someone for the first time. You are bringing in a lot of preconceived ideas and first impressions. But if you want to actually make friends, you have to let go of all that and accept them the way they are.

Likewise, you may have already decided on a design for the stone without having given it the chance to communicate what it "wants." Try to get to know it a little. Pick it up and turn it over in your hand, feeling its weight, its texture, its balance. Or just sit quietly for a while and look at it. After a while, various images will begin to suggest themselves. Perhaps it looks like a church bell; a sea turtle; a geometrical design. Maybe the color calls to mind the solitary wild flower you once saw growing beside a busy highway; and that in turn leads into a whole Macy's parade of ideas which culminate in the perfect design. If you are open to the stone, it will inevitably begin to speak.

You will also begin to discover that you do in fact have your own built-in design sense. You may find that you prefer abstract shapes to the representational ones; or fixed geometric patterns to ones that "move." Some people always make the stone the center of attention, while others like a broad lake-like expanse of silver, broken only occasionally by a bright splash of turquoise. Whatever the style, a design is valid *only* if it works for you.

There is no need to feel, as too many craftsmen do, that you have to come up with a "completely original" design every time you sit down at the drawing board. The rich traditions of the past offer a treasure trove of exciting design ideas which has been mined often and to great effect by artists in the past. Picasso and his contemporaries all freely acknowledged their debt to "primitive" African art. The Art Nouveau movement, perhaps the most wildly innovative period in the history of the jewelry craft, got its impetus from fresh contact with Japanese design concepts. Pattern books, art books, trips to the museum: all will present a broad conceptual runway from which you can take off on your own flights of fancy.

Keeping a notebook and jotting down ideas as they come up will also prove an invaluable help in your designing efforts. Carry the notebook around for a day or two, attempting to look at the world through the special lens of the jewelry designer. Make a sketch of a section of ornamental ironwork in front of an old hotel. Follow the delicate outline of a leaf or the shattered symmetry of a piece of broken bottle glass. In doing so, you will have planted on your pages the seeds for innumerable future projects.

Many jewelers also maintain voluminous collections of simple "doodles," many of which later find their way, in one form or another, into their work. You can spend hours juxtaposing the shape of a stone with a series of rudimentary forms, changing a curve, there adding a line, stepping back occasionally to take a fresh glance. And then, suddenly, something will click. There will be that inexplicable jolt of recognition, that faint tickling of the aesthetic nerve which tells you you've hit on something that "works." The little scrawl, its lines refined and made more definite, may wind up as a magnificent piece of jewelry.

SOME PRACTICAL CONSIDERATIONS

"Form follows function."

Frank Lloyd Wright

Jewelry has taken on a wide variety of forms according to popular fashion in different cultural or historical periods. The modern brooch began its history in Minoan Crete as an oversized diaper pin used for fastening garments. The Aztecs and Egyptians were fond of monstrous, heavy pectorals that would make them a positive hazard in a crowded elevator. In other cultures, jewelry was intended to be encumbering, in order to render the aristocratic wearer, symbolically and otherwise, incapable of doing anything more manual than beckoning the servants.

Aside from modern trends such as "body jewelry," it is a generally accepted axiom today that jewelry should be both comfortable and practical to wear. For example, if it is going to be a brooch, make sure it isn't too heavy and doesn't have too many sharp projections, or it will tear the fabric to which it is pinned. On the other hand, it you are making a design into a buckle, it had better be sturdy enough to withstand the stresses generated by Thanksgiving dinner. And if making a pair of earrings, bear in mind that stretched earlobes, while considered haute couture in some quarters of the globe, have never quite caught on in ours.

From a purely aesthetic standpoint as well, the size and weight of the piece is an important consideration. Some designs call for a delicate feel, while others work better if they are more substantial. Become familiar with the different gauges of sheet and wire which make up the jewelry's "palette." Try to keep a sample of each gauge handy, where you can refer to it when you are trying to decide what to use for a particular piece.

Above all, keep in mind that the design you have drawn must eventually be rendered in metal. Did you think out how and where the fastening will be attached to the body? Is it balanced properly for the way it will hang? Is it structurally sound? Remember that unbacked constructed jewelry should be like a Chinese paper cutting: the design has to stay in one piece. Check to make sure that one of your lines, which may look fine on paper, doesn't wind up cutting a section of the design off the main body.

Many jewelers, in fact, find it helpful to cut the design out of construction paper first before making it in silver. If you can shanghai a cooperative model, you can get an idea how it will look in a position in which it will be worn. You can also determine how a bracelet or a ring shank will appear when it is bent into shape by performing the operation on a cut-out piece of paper in the same pattern. Juxtaposing cut-out shapes in different ways is also a good way of discovering new permutations of the same design. You might even want to try the old third grade show-and-tell project of folding a piece of paper in halves or quarters and cutting into it in different places. Unfolded, it will yield a geometrical pattern which may give you an idea for an attractive piece of jewelry. For those who wish to be thorough, the final design study can be cut from the same gauge brass as the prospective silver design. This is a good way to test the cutting and shaping techniques for a particular pattern.

TOOLS AND TECHNIQUES

If you are going to design your own jewelry, you should begin with the proper tools. Many "non-artists" shy away from trying to make their own designs on the grounds that they "can't draw a straight line." There is a simple solution to that problem: get a ruler. Also buy a few plastic draftsman's templates with graduated series of ovals and circles. You will find that these will help you get the crisp, accurate lines that distinguish the outstanding piece from the mediocre one.

The beauty of jewelry is that anyone who takes the trouble to refine his lines can be a good designer. One highly successful professional describes himself, with a hint of pride, as "nothing more than a glorified doodler." But it is the care he puts into making the simple lines really work that transforms his idle scrawls into technical and artistic tours-de-force.

If you have a pattern which requires several identical shapes, there is a handy trick which will ensure accurate duplication. First, draw one of the shapes on tracing paper with a pencil, 2H or softer. Turn the drawing over, place it over another sheet of paper, and trace over the back. You will leave a mark on the other sheet of paper where you have drawn over the original line. After filling in any gaps where you might have "missed," change the position of the paper with the original drawing and repeat the process until the pattern is complete. Some craftsmen prefer to make a template of a shape for which they would like multiple copies. This can be either cut from twenty-two gauge brass using a jeweler's saw or out of a used X-ray plate with an exacto knife.

It will often be necessary to reduce or enlarge a design. If it is fairly simple, make a basic grid (Figure 8-2) and, duplicating each section of the design piece-by-piece, you will obtain a much more accurate replica than if trying to do it all at once. If the design is a little more complicated, use two pieces of graph paper with different sized boxes (Figure 8-3). The graph paper will also prove helpful in making any kind of symmetrical pattern.

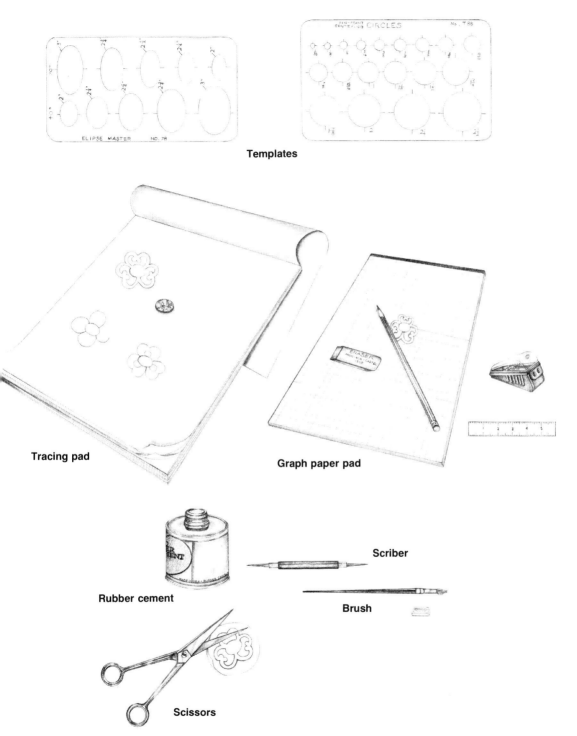

Templates

Tracing pad

Graph paper pad

Rubber cement

Scriber

Brush

Scissors

Figure 8–1.   Proper tools are the beginning of an accurate design.

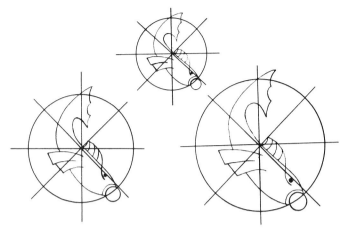

Figure 8–2.   Enlarging a simple design with a basic grid.

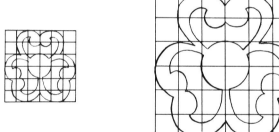

Figure 8–3.   Graded graph paper is useful in enlarging or reducing a design, especially if it is complicated or symmetrical.

It is difficult to over-emphasize the importance of an accurate original design. Constructed jewelry making is like a game of "telephone." As anyone who has ever played knows, if the initial "message" is garbled, what comes out at the other end will be about as clear as dolphin talk. Likewise, any inaccuracies in the original design become greatly magnified as you progress through the various steps in making the piece. Try to make the corrections in the *design,* not the piece.

DESIGN TRANSFER

If you are satisfied with the original design, it is time to transfer it to a piece of silver sheet for sawing. There are various ways to accomplish this, the easiest one being to simply glue the pattern directly onto the silver with rubber cement. This is done as follows:

1. If you didn't draw your original on tracing paper, do so now. #525 is a good weight for this.

2. Cut out an area around the pattern with a scissors, avoiding sharp corners, which will have a tendency to lift off later.

3. Apply a thin coat of rubber cement to both the silver and the back of the pattern. Allow them both to dry for about thirty seconds, then place the paper carefully on the metal. If you have to smooth it down, *don't rub it* with your fingers or you will smudge the pencil lines. Press straight down where needed with your fingers or put a sheet of paper over the pattern and rub gently. Let it dry for about five minutes.

It is important that the paper is pasted down securely. If it lifts off during sawing, your frustration will know no bounds. You will be suddenly left alone in the wilderness of a blank piece of metal without any guide to tell you where you are. It is good practice to wait the extra few minutes to make sure the cement has dried.

There are several other methods which can be used to transfer the design:

1. If you are adept at freehand drawing, you can use a scribe to scratch the design directly onto the metal.

2. You can coat the silver with a thick layer of Chinese white tempera, then draw the design over it *lightly* in pencil (too much extra pressure will cause the pencil to scrape through the paint). Be sure to wash the piece thoroughly before soldering it.

3. A similar method is to again coat the piece with tempera. Then blacken the back of your pattern with a soft pencil. Next, turn the paper over, place it on the piece of painted silver, and go over the lines with a harder pencil. The pattern will be transferred onto the piece (don't try to do this with carbon paper, since the lines will have a nasty tendency to smudge).

Now that you have transferred the design, it's time to talk seriously about sawing it out.

CHAPTER 9

Sawing

". . . When I come to a complicated place, I size up the difficulties, tell myself to watch out and be careful, keep my eyes on what I'm doing, work very slowly, and move the knife with the greatest subtlety . . ."

Chuang Tzu, *The Secret of Caring for Life*

The jeweler's saw is a precision instrument of marvelous capability. Strung with the right blade, it can cut nearly anything in sheet silver that you can draw on paper, from the barest outline to the most extravagant arabesque. At the same time, the tool is almost ridiculously simple—just a handle attached to a steel frame with two clamps to hold the blade taut.

The sawing process is also fairly straightforward. Once you are familiar with a few basic techniques, it's only a matter of guiding the blade carefully along the lines of your design.

Yet for all that, sawing is a uniquely challenging art. Of all the jewelry making techniques, it is less an acquired skill than a moment-to-moment act of awareness. As you will soon discover, the sawblade is extremely sensitive to even the slightest hint of distraction. Even when the blade is hugging the line like a racehorse on the inside track, all it takes is a bit of inattention to send it off the mark. Sawing is the perfect demonstration of Henry David Thoreau's axiom that "the eye may see for the hand, but not for the mind."

To do a proper sawing job, you have to be willing to take your time. The blade can only cut so much metal on each stroke. Speed will only manage to shave a few seconds off your time, and probably mess up your design in the bargain. If you're willing to get into it though, you will find

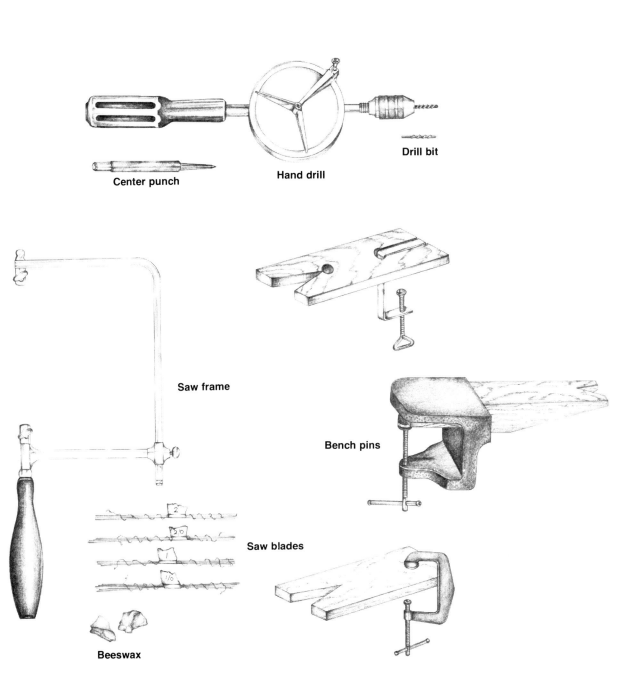

Center punch

Hand drill

Drill bit

Saw frame

Bench pins

Saw blades

Beeswax

Figure 9–1.   Tools for sawing and drilling.

the elephantine pace of the work to be strangely luxurious. Time seems to slow until there is nothing but the here-and-now of the forward edge of the blade, making its steady pilgrim's progress to the end of the line. As the old Indian proverb goes, "Hasten slowly and you will soon arrive." With a little knowledge and a bit of practice there will be no design, however intricate, that you cannot master with your saw.

TOOLS

Saw frames come in a variety of sizes, ranging from two to six inches in depth. The most versatile is a three or four inch one—deep enough to give you room to maneuver, not big enough to be unwieldy. Any make will do; the main consideration is that the clamps, or jaw nuts, are sufficiently well-fitted to hold the blade securely.

Saw blades which are made of fine-tooled tempered steel, are sold in packets of twelve, in gauges which vary from almost the width of a small hacksaw blade (#6) to scarcely coarser than a horse's hair (#8/0). Since all the teeth point down, the sawblade cuts only on the downstroke. At the same time, they are made so that the sides as well as the front have cutting edges, which provides additional maneuverability.

We will mostly be using blades between 3 and 2/0, depending on the project. You will find 1 and 1/0 blades to be the most universally serviceable—fine enough to saw a very accurate line yet thick enough to resist breakage.

Beeswax is used to lubricate the sawblade before use. This helps the blade move more easily through the metal. It also prevents the friction of sawing from heating the blade, and making it brittle.

The bench pin is the basic work surface in the sawing process. The piece of sheet silver is held down with the free hand, straddling the notch, so as to give the saw a free area to cut. A simple home bench pin can be made from a slab of wood with a "V" cut in and fixed to the table with a C-clamp. Many jewelers like to cut smaller grooves or holes into their pins to use when they find it necessary to saw out a really tiny design. A bench pin kit with a fitted clamp included can be purchased in a hardware store or hobby shop. Also available are bench pin/anvil combinations. Though a little more expensive they are useful when needed to flatten out a piece of metal before or after sawing.

The hand drill is used to pierce a hole in the silver through which the sawblade is later inserted. The tiny drill bits (the best sizes being a $1/32$

inch and a ³/₆₄ inch) are placed in the "chuck" at the end of the shaft, then tightened down. As the bits come rather long, it is easier to use them if you break off a piece of the blank end before putting it in the drill. This can be done by clamping the bit into a vise, leaving part of the back end sticking out, and simply knocking it off with a sharp hammer blow. To prepare a piece for drilling, a small depression is made in the metal with a center punch. Center punches in a variety of sizes are available in most hardware stores. A sharp nail will also do the job.

STRINGING THE BLADE

In order to cut most effectively, the saw blade must be strung in the frame under the right amount of tension. Too tight and the blade will have a tendency to snap. Too loose, and it will be difficult to guide.

The following method will usually result in a properly-strung blade:

1. Tighten the blade into the lower clamp, or jaw nut, of the saw frame. Make sure that the teeth are facing *down* and *out*.

2. Adjust the length of the frame so that the blade enters about a third of the way into the upper jaw nut.

3. Push the upper end of the frame against the worktable (the frame is made of spring steel and will give) until the blade is almost all the way to the end of the upper jaw nut (Figure 9-2). Then tighten it down and slowly release the pressure.

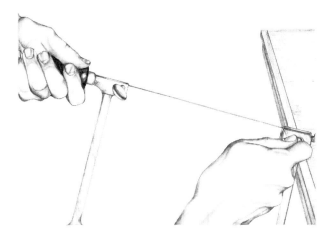

Figure 9–2.   Stringing the blade: push the upper end of the frame against the worktable until the blade is almost all the way to the end of the upper jaw nut.

Some prefer to put the blade in the *upper* end first and tighten it down in the *lower* one. It's basically six of one, half-dozen of the other; whichever one is easiest is right.

Once the blade is tightened, the traditional way to determine if it's ready is to try "playing" it. A well-strung blade, when plucked with a finger, will give a vaguely musical "ping." If it's too tight, it will "plink"; too loose, "plunk." After a while you will be able to hear the subtle difference in tone as well as being able to feel it in the blade.

GUIDING THE SAW (General Maneuvers)

In the process of sawing you should take on something of the attitude of a good English nanny; i.e., firm but gentle guidance. The handle should be gripped loosely, but not to the extent that you can't influence the direction of the blade. Hold the frame completely vertical—the most efficient cutting angle for the downward-slanting teeth—and move it up and down in long, smooth strokes. The important thing to remember is that gravity does the bulk of the work. If you try to push the blade forward, it will be harder to maneuver accurately and much more prone to snap.

The general method of sawing out the design is to follow along the *outer* edge of the line. This not only provides some error insurance, but also compensates for the metal that will be lost in the process of filing.

At a sharp angle in the design, keep the blade moving in place like a jogger waiting for a traffic light, all the while slowly rotating it and/or the sheet of silver in the new direction. Since the sides of the blade are also cutting edges, it will quickly make room for itself to turn around. If you have to back out of a line, just continue the basic up-and-down motion of the blade as you move in reverse.

SAWING OUT THE PATTERN

From the point of view of sawing procedure, there are basically three types of designs. The first is a basic shape, just a simple outline. In this case, the cut is started on the edge of the piece of metal and continued around the outline until the form is sawed out.

A second pattern involves cutting decorative lines into the basic shape (see Projects 2, 8, 13, 14). This is done by following the line in, then backing the blade out again.

The third type consists of both an interior *and* exterior design. The procedure for cutting these is called *piercing* and is done as follows:

1. Using a center punch or an ordinary nail, gently tap a depression into each of the areas to be sawed out (Figure 9-3).

2. Drill holes in the design at these points (Figure 9-4).

3. Thread the sawblade through one of the holes, angling the frame on so the piece of metal comes to rest against the lower jaw nut (Figure 9-5). Using the same basic method described previously, compress the sawframe and tighten down the blade.

4. Cut out the section of silver then detach the blade and repeat the same procedure until all interior parts of the design have been sawed out (Figure 9-6).

5. Cut around the outside of the design (Figure 9-7) until it drops free of the sheet.

Figure 9–3. Piercing: tap a depression into each area.

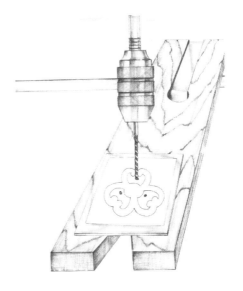

Figure 9–4. Piercing: drill holes.

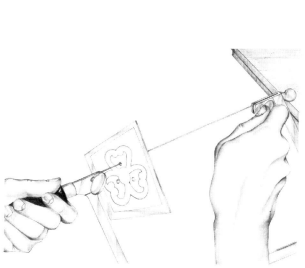

Figure 9–5. Piercing: threading the sawblade through a hole.

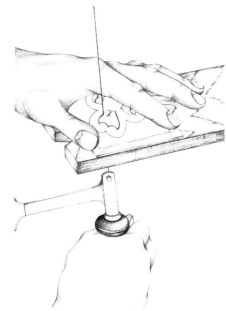

Figure 9–6. Piercing: cutting out a section.

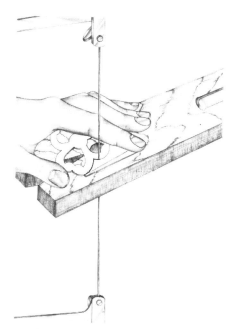

Figure 9–7. Piercing: cutting around the outside.

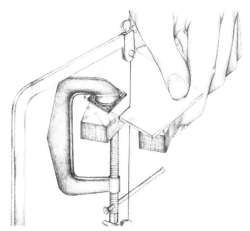

Figure 9–8. Place leather, cork, or cardboard between the clamp and the silver to avoid marring.

HINTS, TRICKS, AND MISCELLANY

• As you saw, metal particles begin to accumulate around the sawcut to such an extent that the design may be obscured. The easiest way to clear these particles is simply to blow them away. This may lead to a rhythm of puffing and sawing that sounds like The Little Engine That Could on a steep grade, but it gets the job done.

• Sometimes you will have a crisis of faith in the midst of your sawing: suddenly those carefully drawn lines just don't look quite right. Before trying to correct them freehand, and possibly ruining a perfectly good design, remember that in sawing just as in life, a certain loss of perspective occurs when you focus your vision on a small area. Step back and think twice before attempting any mid-course corrections.

• Sometimes the piece of metal you are sawing will start to ride with the blade on the upstrokes. Generally, this is a signal that the blade is too hefty for the sheet metal gauge. As a general rule of thumb, three saw teeth per sheet thickness is about right. If you need a thick line in a lighter gauge silver and find yourself running into this problem, hold the piece down with a small C-clamp, taking care to place something— leather, cork, or cardboard—between the clamp and the silver to avoid marring (Figure 9-8).

• If you find the blade has wandered inside the line and you are having trouble guiding it out again, try exerting a gentle *sideways* pressure in the direction of the line as you saw. This brings the cutting edges of that side of the blade into play and will help slip it back across the border. Or stop and move the blade in place until you can turn it.

• To saw out a strip of metal which is longer than the saw frame is deep, take a pair of pliers and bend the part of the blade next to each jawnut until the teeth of the blade are rotated ninety degrees. You will then be able to use the saw sideways, making it possible to cut as long a strip as you like.

CHAPTER 10

Filing

"Work alone will efface the footsteps of work."

James McNeil Whistler

Filing is one of the oldest of all the jewelry making techniques. Before the dawn of the Iron Age and the availability of proper tools, craftsmen were using improvised stone rasps to ingeniously sculpt their design ideas in metal. In fact, prior to the invention of the modern jewelers' saw, even the most intricate patterns were rendered using nothing but crude chisels and a few even cruder files. The startling precision of some of these now priceless museum pieces vividly demonstrates what even the simplest tool can accomplish when it is used creatively.

In modern jewelry, files serve a twofold purpose. On the one hand, filing is a mopping-up operation, a way for the jeweler to correct and refine the basic lines of his piece. In addition, careful filing can create a wide range of decorative effects. A partial listing of the most common usages of the file would include:

1. Smoothing out burrs and serrations left on previously sawed edges

2. Eliminating the visible "join" or seam between two soldered pieces

3. "Truing" and evening out lines and curves

4. Filing decorative patterns, such as scalloped edges, grooves, serrations, etc.

5. Softening edges which might scratch the skin when the piece is worn

6. Beveling edges to create dimension in a flat piece (Figure 10-2)

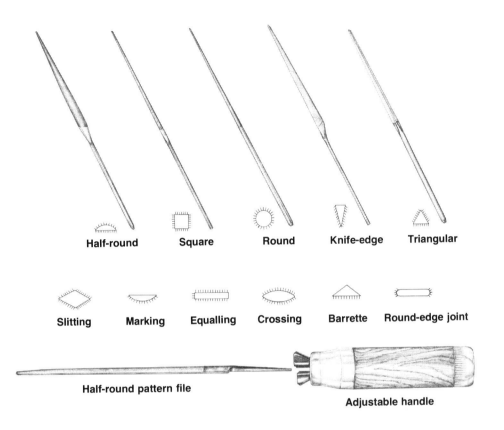

Half-round   Square   Round   Knife-edge   Triangular

Slitting   Marking   Equalling   Crossing   Barrette   Round-edge joint

Half-round pattern file

Adjustable handle

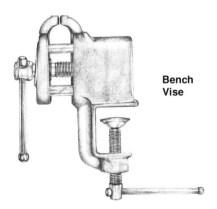

Bench Vise

Figure 10–1.   Files.

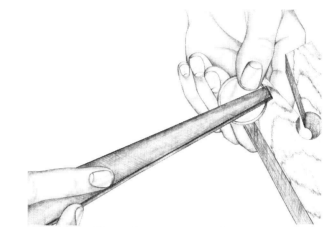

Figure 10–2. Beveling edges to create dimension in a flat piece.

TOOLS

A basic set of files should include at least one large pattern file for quick removal of metal and a set of basic needle files, required for finer work. There are two different classifications of files in use: the American and the Swiss. Swiss files come in grades ranging from 00 (the coarsest) to 8/0 (superfine). The American equivalents are called rough (00), bastard (0), second cut (1), and smooth cut (2), with anything finer being referred to as deadsmooth.

Files are also grouped according to the pattern of the teeth. Single cut files have one row of parallel grooves, and are generally used for finer finishing work. Doublecut (or crosscut) files have another series of lines crossing the first one and are the type most commonly used for precious metals.

Before purchasing any file, you should check to see that it is even by running a finger lightly along the teeth. Some files, particularly the crosscut variety, are essentially just "roughed up" rather than precision tooled, and these will put unnecessary scratches in a jewelry piece.

For the large file in your tool collection, a #2 half-round will probably prove the most versatile. You can get one with a pointed end or the more common blunt end type. Filing will be made much simpler if the file is used with a wooden handle, preferably an adjustable one. Not only does this enhance your control of the file, but the chances of contamination from oil on the hands—which can cause the file to skid—is significantly lessened.

While there is a relatively narrow choice for large pattern files, needle files offer a bewildering array of possibilities. The variety of available shapes suggests some obscure laboratory experiment in the crossbreeding of tools. Some have teeth all over, some have toothed faces and smooth backs, and some have teeth only on the edges. Every eventuality seems to have been thought of by the manufacturers and many jewelers become collectors of files just for the sheer fascination of it.

For our purposes, however, a few basic shapes will suffice. The bottom line is one half-round, one flat, and one round (rat-tail) needle file, all #2 cut. Creatively used, these will address most of your filing needs. You will also eventually want to purchase at least a knife edge (for cutting V-grooves), a four-square (for truing corners) and a triangular (or three-square).

Other future additions to your file collection might include: riffler (die-sinker) files, which could be called the jeweler's dental tools—their curved ends are excellent for getting into hard to reach spots; and a checkering file, frequently used by Zuni and other Indian craftsmen to make decorative serrations on bezels, wire, etc. It would also be very useful to go out and get an inexpensive garden or lawnmower file to use for filing jobs involving epoxy or other substances you would prefer not to clog your good files with.

A small bench vise of some sort is also almost indispensable for filing. All sorts of models are available, from deluxe ones with built-in anvils to your basic pair of jaws. The inexpensive variety will be perfectly adequate for our purposes—if the finished piece is good, the make, model, or price of the equipment used is irrelevant.

When used to hold a piece of silver, the jaws must be covered to protect the work. This can be done by wrapping a piece of chamois cloth or soft leather around each jaw and securing it with a rubber band, or by gluing strips of thin cork or other material to the jaw faces with contact cement.

TECHNIQUES

Due to the angle of the teeth, the cutting action of the file takes place *only* on the forward stroke. Generally, the most effective filing motion is one which starts at the tip and goes the whole length of the file. In the case of large files, the free hand can be used to guide the stroke as well as to keep the teeth in contact with the metal (Figure 10-3). Pressure should

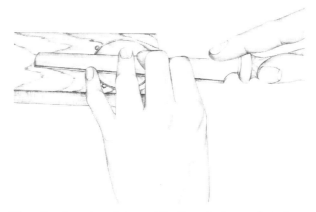

Figure 10–3.   Use the free hand to guide the stroke and to keep the teeth in contact with the metal.

be gentle, however; too much downward force will just slow the file without adding to its cutting power. On the return stroke, the file should either be lifted off the piece entirely or allowed to slide back lightly to avoid dulling the teeth.

In general, inattention is the disaster of filing. Always pay heed to what the thing is doing. If trying to eliminate a high spot, make sure you are not, at the same time, making a valley where a mountain once was. If you have been filing in one direction for some time, check to see that parallel grooves are not developing in the metal. If they are, the direction of the filing process should be rotated by ninety degrees. Always try to avoid creating new problems in the course of solving old ones!

HINTS

1. When filing a flat piece, it is helpful to pound a few carpet tacks into your work surface just below the level of the metal to hold the piece in place (Figure 10-3).

2. When filing an edge even on a larger work, clamp the piece in your bench vise. This has the added advantage of leaving both hands free to guide the file (Figure 10-4).

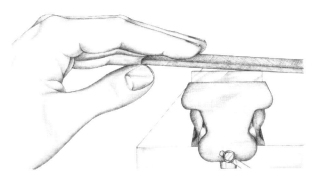

Figure 10–4. When filing an edge on a larger work, clamp the piece in a bench vise.

3. A ring clamp (see Figure 12-1) is especially useful for holding pieces which might be too small or fragile to hold by hand.

4. If the area to be filed is quite large, it is more practical to use a broad stroke which moves crossways and forwards at the same time. If filing an edge which has high spots, use a sweeping diagonal stroke rather than following along the line of the edge—this will cover the most ground most evenly. Also, use the flat side of a file on the outside of curves, reserving the rounded side for the inside lines.

5. In general after filing a piece, always remember to give the top and bottom edges a light once-over to remove any burr that may have formed (Figure 10-5). If not taken off, this will later impede proper solder flow. Filing it away at a slight angle, on the other hand, creates a bead along which the solder will run smoothly.

Figure 10–5. After filing a piece, always give the top and bottom edges a light once-over to remove burrs.

CARE OF THE FILE

Files should be treated as you would any other precision tool. They should be kept in a clean, dry place to avoid rust. They should not be thrown into the same drawer where rubbing together will eventually dull them (a good needle file holder can be made by drilling a few rows of slightly angled holes into a small block of wood and inserting them handle first for easy identification and access).

In the course of your work, bang the edge of the file against the workbench periodically to dislodge metal particles from the teeth. Dusting the teeth with ordinary blackboard chalk is a useful preventative—it will keep out excess metal without clogging the teeth.

In addition, files should be thoroughly cleaned at regular intervals. Hobby shops carry wire brushes called file cards which are made for this purpose. The bristles should be brushed across, not along, the length of the file. Particularly stubborn matter can be scraped from the teeth with a pointed tool or ordinary straight pin.

CHAPTER 11

Soldering

"First, to be comparatively small. Secondly, to be smooth. Thirdly, to have variety in the direction of the parts; but fourthly, to have those parts not angular but melted as it were into each other."

Edmunde Burke,
"On the Sublime and the Beautiful"
1756

Soldering is magic. Anyone who tells you differently has probably never done it. Through a process which falls just short of alchemy, the individual elements of the design are suddenly fused together, synthesized into a new whole. If all's gone well, you've created something with as good a chance of weathering the eons as King Tut's sarcophagus.

Thrilling though soldering is, it also contains a certain element of high drama. Once you begin heating the piece, you can't be sure of the outcome until you've finished. The parts may melt together as if they were destined for each other; or they may just sit there, as interested in mingling as two plaintiffs at a divorce hearing. The results depend totally on three factors: good preparation, careful heating, and a thorough knowledge of the soldering process.

The soldering itself is not really that complicated. Silver solder (the word comes from the Latin for "to make solid") is simply a lower melting alloy of silver. When placed between two pieces of metal and heated, it liquifies and flows between the surfaces in much the same way water does when pressed between two panes of glass. As soon as the heat is removed, the solder instantaneously hardens, or "freezes," holding the pieces together like some sort of metallic Krazy Glue.

The tools for soldering are generally not very elaborate; all that is really

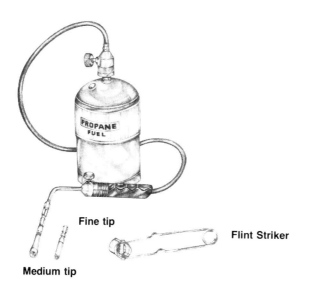

Fine tip

Flint Striker

Medium tip

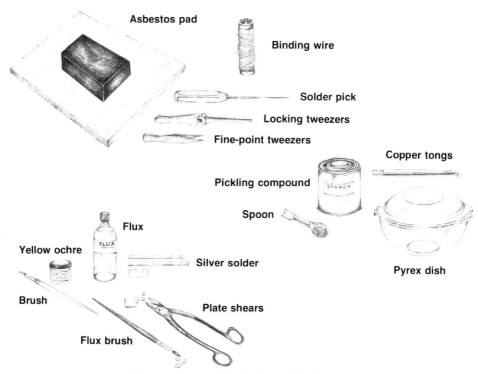

Asbestos pad

Binding wire

Solder pick

Locking tweezers

Fine-point tweezers

Copper tongs

Pickling compound

Spoon

Flux

Yellow ochre

Silver solder

Pyrex dish

Brush

Plate shears

Flux brush

Figure 11–1.   Tools for soldering.

required is a good soldering surface and a steady source of heat. An ordinary propane hand torch will do fine, but if you can find it, it's better to purchase one with a rubber hose and torch handle assembly. These are easier to hold than the kind with the nozzles attached directly to the tank, with the added advantage of a generally more steady flame. Ronson also makes a small torch which fits in the hand a little more gracefully than some of the other brands. In either case, you should get a small fine point (pin-point) tip for more delicate soldering operations.

The best soldering surface is a charcoal block, which is obtainable at any jewelry supply shop. Although you will sometimes see jewelers using ordinary firebrick, these have a tendency to dissipate heat, prolonging the soldering process. Charcoal blocks do have a tendency to crack, but this can be effectively prevented by wrapping them with fifteen or twenty turns of iron binding wire, also available in a craft store. Restaurant grill-cleaning blocks (the natural pumice kind) and bismuth blocks also make excellent soldering surfaces. A quarter inch asbestos pad is used under the block to protect the work surface in your shop.

Although there are a variety of other soldering tools, these would be most easily understood in terms of the various processes, which can be divided into the following steps:

1. cleaning the pieces;

2. fitting them to make proper contact;

3. applying a flux (a chemical which allows the solder to flow);

4. placing the solder at the contact points between the pieces;

5. soldering the whole assembly together using the torch.

Finally, the piece is "pickled" in a mild acid solution to remove surface discolorations resulting from the heating process. An understanding of each one of these steps is absolutely essential, and we would do well to take the time to examine them one by one.

CLEANING

Dealing with solder is a little like dealing with a cranky old gentleman boarder. You know that if everything isn't arranged just so—sheets clean, room in order, temperature just right—you can expect to hear about it. After a while, you realize it's easier to accommodate an idiosyncrasy rather than trying to ignore it.

As far as solder is concerned, cleanliness is next to godliness. If either the surfaces of the metal or the solder is dirty when it comes time for it to melt, the solder will just roll up in a finicky little ball and refuse to budge. Although some jewelers clean off offending grease or oxide film by heating the piece and then quenching it in acid, rubbing it with or over some 1/0 emery paper (Figure 11-2) is a perfectly adequate alternative. You will be able to tell it is clean by its shininess. Solder strips are cleaned with a small piece of folded emery paper (Figure 11-3).

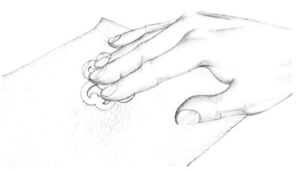

Figure 11–2. Before soldering, clean off grease or oxide film by rubbing the piece over some 1/0 emery paper.

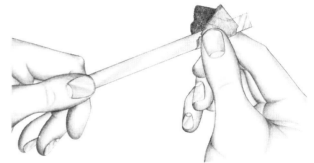

Figure 11–3. Solder strips are cleaned with a small, folded piece of emery paper.

FITTING

A close fit between the parts is an essential requirement for a good join. Solder will only flow between two surfaces which are actually touching. It will *not* fill in a gap. It may therefore be necessary to play around with the pieces a little, bending them here and there as needed, until a good fit is obtained. If two edges are to be joined (referred to as a "butt" joint), they must be filed even. Wire should be rubbed over emery paper until the bottom is slightly flat and makes good contact with the surface to which it is to be soldered. Check to see that the pieces fit flush by holding them up to the light or examining them at eye level for any gaps in contact.

Sometimes a poorly-fitted piece will soften under heat enough to settle into place. A pointed tool may also be used to carefully press down parts during soldering. However, relying on either one of these is risky business. It is far better to take the time to get everything lined up right before lighting the torch.

FLUXING

Flux, as the name implies, is used to facilitate the flow of solder. In other days, flux recipes called for ingredients ranging from the "fat of an old sow" (medieval) to "burnt wine sediments" (an old Greek favorite). As members of the trade began to lose interest in chasing pigs and cleaning up after bacchanals, new substances were devised, culminating with today's easy-to-use fluxes.

All parts of the work which are to be joined, as well as the solder itself, *must* be coated with flux. This creates an oxygen resistant film, which prevents solder-impeding oxides from forming on the surface of the piece during heating.

There are two basic types of flux: borax fluxes, which, when heated, form a layer of fused borax glass over the piece; and the fluoron-based fluxes. For the purposes of this book, Battern's Self-Picking Flux, a fluoron-based solution, is recommended for its ease of use. It comes in the form of a green liquid which is applied with an ordinary camel's hair brush. When using fluoron fluxes, it is important to have some ventilation; at least a window opened a crack. The fumes, though not particularly dangerous, should nonetheless not be inhaled for prolonged periods of time.

SOLDER PLACEMENT

Solder placement is strategic. The objective is to cover all the territory with the smallest possible deployment of forces. The tin soldiers in this case are tiny snippets of solder around 1/32 inch or so square. They are made by first fringing the end of the solder strip with metal cutting

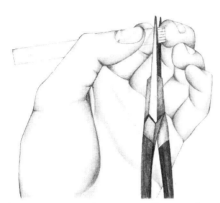

Figure 11–4. Place your finger along the edge of the shears to keep tiny snippets of solder from flying in every direction.

Figure 11–5. Another way to hold onto the tiny pieces of solder is to snip them into your cupped palm.

scissors (plate shears) and then cutting across the lines. You would be well-advised to place a finger along the edge of the shears (Figure 11-4) or cup your hand (Figure 11-5) to keep the cut pieces from flying out at random.

The snippets are placed by picking them up with a flux-moistened brush tip and depositing them, with a wiping motion, on the piece (Fig-

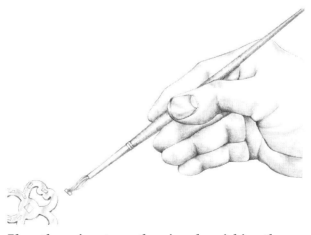

Figure 11–6. Place the snippets on the piece by picking them up with a flux-moistened brush tip.

ure 11-6). It is helpful to trim the brush to a point with a pair of ordinary scissors to make accurate placement of smaller pieces a little easier. The tip should also be wiped on the lip of the bottle before picking up the solder to avoid getting too much extra flux on the piece. Puddles tend to swell into fungus-like mounds when heat is applied. If you do happen to apply too much, the brush tip can be squeezed out and used to blot up the excess liquid.

There are various ways of placing solder, depending on the requirements of a particular piece. In "sweat soldering"—the most commonly used technique for constructed jewelry—solder is essentially "sandwiched" between the pieces to be joined. This is done by first applying the snippets to the back of the top piece, and then, after the flux has dried them in place, setting it down on the base.

The primary consideration should always be that the solder makes contact with all surfaces which are to be joined. If wire is to be soldered to sheet, for example, the snippets are placed leaning against the wire so that they are touching both the wire and the base. In situations where placing solder in the usual manner might prove awkward, snippets can be pre-melted in place in the appropriate spots before the elements of the piece are set in position.

When deciding how much solder to use, remember this rule of thumb: solder will generally spread out to cover *two to three* times its own surface area when melted. This will help you visualize what quantity to place where. Special attention must be paid to any projecting parts of the design. This may mean lots of little snippets, but the trouble you take at this point will be worth it to ensure a good join. Also, keep in mind that the bigger the piece of solder, the more heat it will take to melt it. A single piece of solder, generally, should never be larger than ⅛ inch square.

THE SOLDERING OPERATION

Soldering your piece of jewelry can be compared to the launching of a space shot. The piece is placed on the "launching pad," the "rockets" ignited, and if everything proceeds as it should from there, Mission Control can start popping corks. If not, as Werner von Braun used to say, "Back to the drawing board."

1) *Preflight Briefing*

Solder comes from the manufacturer in three different grades: *easy* (not to be confused with "soft," which is a low-melting lead-based solder), *medium*, and *hard*. Each one has a different melt and flow point, which makes it possible to perform multiple solderings on the same piece without remelting the previously soldered joins. (It is a good idea to label each strip by scratching an "H," "M," or "E" to avoid mix-ups.)

You *can* use the same grade several times running; remelting solder, like life's other minor vices, is not particularly harmful unless you overdo it. In fact, since it takes more heat to melt the same grade a second time, with cautious heating you may avoid the whole problem. However, keep in mind that each time it is remelted, the join becomes more porous, and, as a result, progressively weaker. Therefore, consider three times the absolute maximum number of remeltings of the same join unless you want to risk the whole thing coming apart at the seams later.

Which grade to use depends on the individual piece. You have to make a mental battle plan in advance taking into account how many solderings the piece requires overall, which of them involves delicate pieces which could melt if heated too much, etc. Taking a moment to examine the following chart might be helpful:

	Melts	Flows
Easy	1145	1205
Medium	1275	1360
Hard	1365	1450
Sterling Silver	1640	

The numbers are not terribly important. More important are the relationships between them. For example, hard solder is the closest to the melting point of silver (which begins to "break down" above 1500 degrees); except where necessary, it should be used sparingly by beginners until they get the hang of the whole process. Remember, all grades of silver solder are referred to generically as "hard" solder, and any one of them makes a join which, unless you happen to live in the Towering Inferno, should hold up well under your normal daily routine.

You will also notice from the chart that all the solder grades have both a melt *and* a flow point. Although knowing the actual temperatures is not necessary, you should be aware of the fact. Basically, this means that it is necessary to continue heating a few seconds after the solder melts to make sure it spreads out enough to create a good join.

Solder has another interesting property: it will always flow to the hottest part of the piece. This has its advantages and drawbacks. On the positive side, the solder can be drawn into areas where it is needed by leading it with the torch flame. On the cautionary side, it means that if the piece has been heated unevenly, the solder will also flow unevenly, leaving spots which are not properly joined.

2) *The Launch Site*

Before doing any soldering, you must prepare your soldering area. First, you will need a "pickling" solution to drop the piece into when the soldering process is done. Its purpose is basically to remove the oxide coat or "firescale" which accumulates during soldering. Although many professional jewelers use nitric acid and water (aqua regia) this is somewhat dangerous and not really necessary. Jewelry supply shops carry a granulated dry compound called Sparex which is almost as effective. It is very similar in composition to household toilet cleaner, and is much safer to use. The Sparex should be mixed with water in a shallow pyrex dish and placed within easy reach. If you have a hotplate handy, put the dish on that and heat the pickle before soldering. This will greatly enhance the action of the chemical.

Directly in front of you should be the charcoal block, resting on a pad of asbestos. Also, within reach should be a soldering pick (which can be used for pressing lightly on recalcitrant pieces or even drawing solder into a seam where it is needed); a pair of locking tweezers, for picking up the hot piece; and a pair of copper tongs, for lifting it out. Do not under any circumstances allow the tweezers to come into contact with the Sparex solution; this will cause a chemical reaction which will put an unwanted coating of copper on any piece dropped into it. A bent length of copper electrical wire with the insulation stripped off the ends will make an adequate pair of home-made tongs. A pair of fine-point tweezers will prove useful whenever you have to move small pieces around.

3) *Countdown, Ignition, Lift-Off*

Finally, the moment of truth. The pieces are sawed, filed, cleaned, and fluxed, the solder is placed, the piece is sitting expectantly on the charcoal block. Sit back for a minute and take one last look at it before it becomes posterity. Is everything *just* the way you want it? Because that's how it will be. Soldering, remember, is a marriage of metals, an exchange of vows on the molecular level which is more easily made than broken. Unsoldering is tricky: it can be done, but it will leave a scar on the piece.

Once you are satisfied, light the torch. This is best done with a flint striker rather than a match—they are safer, easier, good for hundreds of lights, and available for under a dollar at the hardware store. Since with propane torches, the gas tends to spurt out rather fast, just turn the knob a crack—you will have all you need.

The cardinal rule of soldering is *steady and even heating.* The entire piece must be brought up to soldering temperature before the solder will melt. Any cold spots will just draw heat away. In heating a heavier piece, a few lengths of bent coathanger wire placed between it and the block will enable you to direct the flame from underneath as well as from above. This is especially helpful when delicate parts are being soldered to larger ones, as heating from below minimizes the risk of melting the top pieces.

To begin heating the piece, direct the flame at the air just above it. This will evaporate any moisture left in the flux (if wet, flux can send solder snippets popping off the piece like so many Mexican jumping beans). Next, begin to play the torch directly over the piece with a rapid figure-eight motion, using the tip of the middle core of the flame (Figure 11-7).

Figure 11–7. Play the torch directly over the piece with a rapid figure-eight motion, using the tip of the middle core of the flame.

If the bottom piece is thicker than the top, you should direct the flame more at that to even out the heat. As the piece is gradually brought up to soldering temperature, you can direct the flame at a particular area of the piece where it seems to be needed, but never for very long. To reiterate, even heating is almost always the most effective.

It is helpful to do all soldering in dim light. Besides being rather romantic, it makes it easier to see the color changes which indicate which stage the piece has reached in the heating process. At first, you will notice a greyish-red cast. In true watched-pot fashion, nothing of much consequence will happen until the piece reaches a uniform dull red, at which point the solder will suddenly begin to melt (if two pieces of sheet are being joined, this will be evidenced by the top one suddenly "dropping"). Continue heating. When the entire construction reaches a color between dull and bright red, the solder should flow, a bright seam of molten solder showing at the edges of the top piece. *Stop* heating. If you go much past this stage, it will turn a cherry-red (the danger zone) and then begin to visibly break down.

4) Mid-Course Corrections

If the solder isn't melting when it should have, there are a number of possible explanations:

1. The piece was heated too fast, exhausting the capabilities of flux to protect the piece from the solder's mortal enemy—surface oxidation.

2. The piece was heated too slowly, doing the same thing.

3. The solder found the piece a little too dirty for its liking.

4. The pieces were not fitted properly.

If the solder has curled up into a recalcitrant little ball, you can sometimes (once the piece has been brought up to soldering temperature) momentarily zero in with the flame to encourage melting. If this doesn't do it, you had better throw up your hands and abort the mission. Especially if using the hard grade solder, capitulate gracefully—it will be about as responsive as an armadillo that has been poked with a stick, and if you manage to get it to flow, all you will achieve is a classic Pyrrhic victory—the entire piece will melt along with it.

If the pieces won't drop, you can try using your soldering pick to very gently press on the top, but be careful—although this often works, metal at this temperature has little structural consistency, and is prone to breakage. If the solder has melted but not flowed into the join it was intended for, you can try inserting the pick into the melted solder and "drawing" it into the right place as you heat.

5) *Splash-Down*

Once you've done all you can do, you should quench the piece in pickle solution. Grip it securely in your locking tweezers and drop it into the pyrex dish, taking care not to let the ends of the tweezers come into contact with the solution. If the piece was rather large, allow it to air cool for one to two minutes. Otherwise, the sudden change in temperature can cause it to crack, which will be your very own disaster movie. If some of the pieces come off in the pickle solution, it is probably because the top piece was allowed to get too much hotter than the bottom, and the solder, being what it is, flowed in the direction of the heat source rather than joining the pieces together.

At any rate, allow the piece to sit in the pickle until it turns "dead white," then lift it out with the copper tongs and see what you have wrought. You should then rinse the pickle off under a running faucet. This is done for two reasons: for one thing, Sparex is an acid solution, albeit mild, and can irritate the skin; also, in a piece which calls for multiple solderings, it will impede the flow of solder.

FIRESCALE

Firescale (also called firestain, firecoat) is a black or reddish skin which forms on the piece due to the oxidation of the copper present in sterling silver. The surface coating of cupric oxide can be removed by leaving the piece in pickle—this will dissolve the copper, leaving a thin coat of fine (pure) silver. Cup*rous* oxide is another problem. The result of overheating, it will show up during the polishing process as a deep purplish-red discoloration.

There are two ways of dealing with this deeper firestain. One is to buff it off on the polishing machine (see Chapter 15). This will take time, as the firestain has generally penetrated to a good depth, and may also wind up removing a good deal of metal. Another—essentially cosmetic—solution is done as follows:

1. Heat the piece to a dull red and quench it in hot pickle. This will bring up a thin layer of fine silver on the piece.

2. Buff the piece lightly.

3. Repeat this process three times. The piece will acquire a thin disguising coat of fine silver. Care must be taken, however, not to remove this during polishing.

ADDITIONAL TOOLS AND TECHNIQUES

1) Flame-Texturing and Fusing

These are two techniques—one a surface embellishment, the other a joining process—used to produce interesting textural effects on a piece. Each requires heating the silver almost to the melting point, and is definitely not recommended for the faint of heart!

In flame-texturing, the piece is fluxed and the torch played over it until it passes the cherry-red stage. The surface will pucker, creating a flowing, oddly Dali-esque surface texture.

In fusing, the piece is fluxed and covered with small pieces of scrap, shot, or wire, then heated until the silver turns orange with dancing highlights. At some point just before the silver begins to melt, the small pieces fuse to the surface, creating an interesting, molten-looking design. Silver filings applied in the same way will result in a fairly good imitation of a sand cast finish.

2) Yellow Ochre

It has been said that everything in the universe has its opposite, and for flux it is a compound called yellow ochre. Ochre is used to *prevent* the flow of solder, either to protect previously soldered joins, or to prevent solder from flowing onto a particular part of the design. The ochre, which comes in powder form and is mixed with water to form a paste, does its work by both dirtying the surface over which the solder would flow and absorbing heat. Jewelers are about evenly divided on its usefulness in relation to the trouble it can sometimes be to clean it off. The best thing would be to experiment with it yourself and come to your own conclusions. It can be removed using a solution of hot water, household ammonia, and dishwashing detergent.

3) *Third Hand and Carbon Mandrel*

These are two useful extra tools you will want to purchase at some point. There are two different kinds of third hands: one is simply a locking tweezers mounted with ball joint on metal stand. The other consists of a similarly mounted pair of alligator clips. They are used for holding pieces in a vertical position during soldering. The same thing can be accomplished by resting your locking tweezers on a raised surface such as piece of ordinary brick. The carbon mandrel, a tapered carbon cone on a stand, is a handy way to solder rings (see Project 4).

4) *Mapp Gas, Cleanburn*

These new high temperature fuels come in cannisters which can be fitted with any conventional propane nozzle. A composition of methyl acetylene propadiene, they maintain a stable high temperature which burns over 800 degrees hotter than propane. They are recommended for projects such as belt buckles where the thickness of the metal makes the use of simple propane tedious, if not impossible.

Many people approach the whole subject of soldering with some trepidation. Most worries, though, are basically groundless, based more on the prospect of doing something unfamiliar than any real danger. Correctly performed, soldering is scarcely any more risky than frying the morning bacon and eggs over the flame of the stove. At the same time, it would be good to observe a few simple precautions:

1. Do not wear flammable clothing (acrylics are a prime offender) when soldering.

2. Always keep the torch pointed away from you or anything flammable. Propane torches in particular have a tendency to keep burning for a few seconds after you shut them off. Some jewelers nail a piece of brass with a nozzle-sized hole in it to the workbench, so the torch can be set down out of the way immediately after soldering.

3. Solder with your legs spread slightly apart so if you drop a hot piece of metal, it won't land in your lap.

4. Above all, respect the flame, but don't be afraid of it. Handling it in too gingerly a manner is also dangerous, as it will make it more difficult to control. Take your time, watch what you're doing, have some confidence, and you will find soldering to be an enjoyable, even stirring, experience.

CHAPTER 12

Setting Turquoise

"There is no substitute for a good fit."

Tailor's Motto

"We Do Alterations."

Ibid.

Stone setting, like good tailoring, is the art of making things fit. In this case, the purpose is to get a fine silver strip called a bezel to fit so gracefully around a chunk of turquoise that the two look as if they came out of the ground together.

Some varieties of the stone—Persian and, increasingly, treated—are commonly available in calibrated rounds and ovals. These can be fitted, so to speak, right off the rack. The irregular shapes present a little more of a challenge. But their bold assymmetry, heightened by a thin line of flashing silver, is an exciting design concept.

Commercial bezel wire is available from any jewelry supply shop, in sizes ranging from $1/16$ to $3/8$ of an inch wide. You can ask the salesperson to cut a strip the length desired. You can also purchase a small sheet of thin gauge fine silver, if the store carries it, and make your own. Although some jewelers cut their bezel strips out of 26 or 28 gauge sterling, the beginner will find it easier to work with than those made from the much softer fine silver.

MEASURING THE BEZEL

The first step in measuring the bezel is deciding on the bezel width you

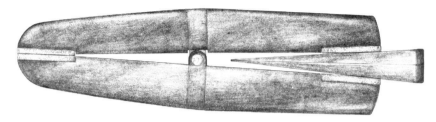

Ring clamp

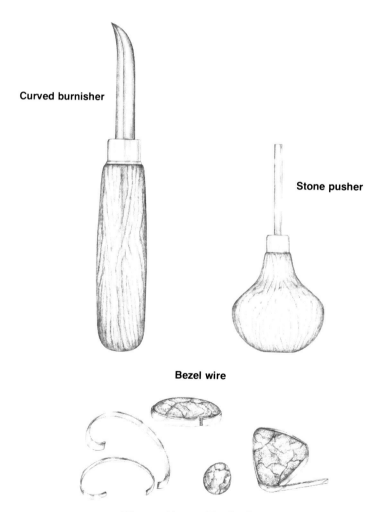

Curved burnisher

Stone pusher

Bezel wire

Figure 12–1.   Tools for setting.

need. This is determined in the same way that Goldilocks figured out which chair to sit in to eat the bears' breakfast: "Too high, too low, just right" (Figure 12-2). The general rule is that the bezel should come up to about one-third the height of the cabochon. If none of the standard sizes are right, cut some of the strip away with the plate shears. Then file the

Figure 12–2. Trying different bezel widths: too high, too low, just right.

edge clean of any burrs or ragged spots left by this procedure, since they will detract from the setting. Unevenly domed cabs are a little trickier (Figure 12-3A). Unless it is altered, when it is pushed up against the turquoise the bezel will look like a hand-me-down suit. Parts of it will overlap the surface, other parts will not come up high enough, and the outline of the stone when viewed from above will appear generally distorted.

The way around this is as follows: 1) fit the bezel around the stone; 2) mark off the spots where it needs to be changed; 3) cut these areas away with the shears (Figure 12-3B,3C). Remember to make the free ends of the bezel the same height so they can be soldered together evenly.

If the stone is lentile-shaped, you can, after the bezel is soldered, raise it up with a piece of wire (Figure 12-4A) or a few pieces of cardboard cut

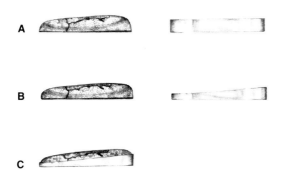

A

B

C

Figure 12–3. Cutting a bezel to fit an unevenly domed cab.

to size. A similar technique can be used with a too-thin piece of turquoise (Figure 12-4B). Many jewelers prefer to put a little sawdust in the bottom of the bezel instead. It accomplishes the same thing, and has the added advantage of cushioning the stone.

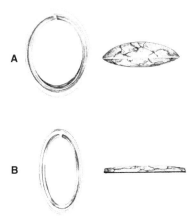

Figure 12–4. If the stone is lentile-shaped or too thin, you can raise it with a few pieces of wire.

There are several methods of determining the length of the bezel. One is to simply wrap some bezel wire tightly around the stone, make a mark just short of where the ends overlap (Figure 12-5), and cut with the saw

Figure 12–5. One simple way to determine the length of the bezel is to wrap some bezel wire tightly around the stone and mark just short of where the ends overlap.

or with special metal-cutting scissors (plate shears) which can be purchased at the jewelry supply or hardware store. You can use a strip of
heavy construction paper in a similar manner. In general, it is better to
make the bezel too tight than too loose, since it can be stretched a little
after soldering.

If the stone is a regular, calibrated size, you can simply compute how
much bezel wire is needed. For ovals the formula is ½ (height plus
width) + bezel thickness (generally 1-2mm); for rounds, (diameter × 3.14)
+ bezel thickness.

SOLDERING THE BEZEL TOGETHER

Before soldering the ends together, they must be filed flush so they
will make a good join. They are then tension-fitted together by rubbing
them past each other until enough "spring" has built up to hold them
securely pressed together (Figure 12-6). Don't worry if you have to make

Figure 12–6.   Build up "spring" by rubbing the bezel ends past one another.

the bezel into an oval in order to make the ends meet properly—the
metal is easily reshaped after soldering. Squeezing the ends together
with flat-nose pliers will help the final alignment (Figure 12-7).

The bezel is next placed on the charocal block and fluxed, and a piece
of hard solder is placed where edges join (Figure 12-8). A small torch tip
should be used to avoid melting the bezel. Remember to move the flame
around rather than concentrating the heat on the piece of solder: bezels

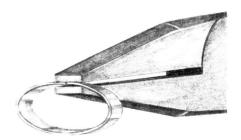

Figure 12–7. Squeezing the ends of the bezel together with flat-nosed pliers will help the final alignment.

Figure 12–8. Place a piece of hard solder where the edges join.

melt rather easily! After soldering, the bezel is opened again by slipping it onto a ring mandrel (Figure 13-1). In the case of a really small bezel, a nail, wooden dowel or similar object can be used. A $9/16$ inch drift punch is particularly handy for this. After soldering, the seam is filed with a needle file until the line is no longer visible.

When it is soldered, the bezel is tried on for size. It should fit the stone snugly but not too snugly. *Don't try to force it.* Remember that turquoise, particularly turquoise with matrix, is prone to crack under stress. If you start to feel like the fat lady with the girdle, quit while you're ahead. The bezel can be enlarged by putting it on the ring mandrel and giving it a few light taps around the circumference with a rawhide hammer (Figure 12-9). You can also stretch it by rolling it over the work surface with a large nail or a dowel. If the bezel is too big, cut out the seam and try again.

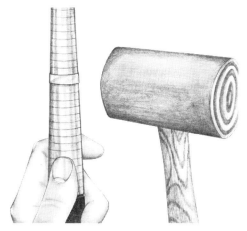

Figure 12–9.   The bezel can be enlarged by putting it on the ring mandrel and tapping it lightly with a rawhide hammer.

MAKING BEZEL CUPS

The bezel cup is one of the basic units of constructed jewelry-making. It is made as follows:

1. Rub the bezel over a piece of 1/0 sandpaper to clean the bottom edge for soldering (Figure 12-10). This may distort the shape a little, so "true" it by inserting the stone.

2. Flux a piece of 18 or 20 gauge scrap silver, set the bezel in position, and place four snippets of medium solder inside it as shown in Figure 12-11.

3. Carefully heat the piece until the solder melts, keeping the flame moving. At no time should you allow the flame to focus on the bezel. When the solder melts, play the flame around the outside of the seam to draw the solder into the join. Try to make sure that all the solder has melted before removing the heat. Any lumps along the inside edge of the bezel can make it difficult for the stone to seat properly.

4. After pickling the piece, cut around the edge of the bezel with the saw, being careful not to saw into the bezel itself. (Figure 12-12).

Figure 12–10. Making bezel cups: First rub the bezel over a piece of 1/0 sandpaper to clean the bottom edge for soldering.

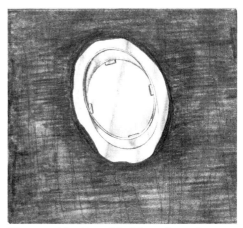

Figure 12–11. Making bezel cups: Evenly distribute four snippets of medium solder inside the bezel.

The bezel cup can be mounted on a ring as it is or used as a unit in other jewelry pieces.

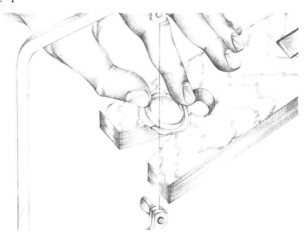

Figure 12–12. Making bezel cups: Saw around the edge of the bezel, being careful not to cut into the bezel itself.

SETTING THE STONE

Meanwhile, at our tailor shop, the customer returns to try on the suit.

Naturally, one question is paramount in everyone's mind: will it fit? If the bezel is too big for the stone, there's not much that can be done. However, once the bezel is pushed into place, the problem may not be noticeable.

If it is too small, you are faced with a dieter's choice: enlarge the clothes or shrink the waistline. For once, the nobler path is also the easiest. Although you can file away a little of the inside wall of the bezel, rasping away a little of the outside bottom edge of the stone with a diamond nailfile (the drugstore variety) will also help the stone to slip into the setting.

Before going any further, you should make sure there are no unmelted lumps of solder lounging against the inside edge of the bezel. If there are, try scraping them away with the end of a file or a curved burnisher tip (Figure 12-13).

The curved burnisher and the stone pushing tool are used to set the stone into the bezel. The burnisher can assume more positions than a ballerina, all of which will help in creating that smooth, tight line around

Figure 12–13.   Scrape away unmelted lumps of solder with a curved burnisher tip.

the stone that is so essential to the aesthetic impact of the work. A stone pushing tool also comes in handy, especially when bezeling settings on a flat piece (Figure 12-14). Some jewelers use the stone pusher to press the

Figure 12–14.   A stone pusher is handy when bezeling settings on a flat piece.

bezel up against the stone and then use the burnisher for smoothing it out. Others use one for all functions. Since they are both relatively inexpensive, it would be worth the investment to try them both out and see which you prefer for what. There are also ring clamps which hold the shank of a ring between the jaws at one end by wedging the opposite end; this is useful in holding ring mounts during bezeling.

The first step in setting the stone is "crimping" the bezel in eight places around its circumference (Figure 12-15). Always alternate from one side to the opposite to avoid "bunching up." Then go around the outside edge of the bezel, gradually forcing the metal closer and closer to the stone in a smoothing motion. Some jewelers insist that the side of the

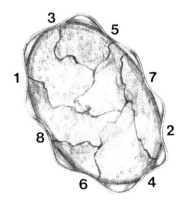

Figure 12–15.   Setting the stone: first crimp the bezel in eight places.

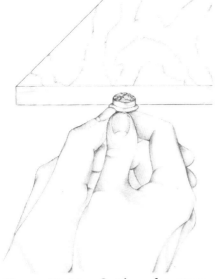

Figure 12–16. Setting the stone: use the side of the worktable to gradually force the metal closer to the stone.

Figure 12–17. Setting the stone: press the top of the bezel closer to the stone, using the outside edge of the burnisher.

worktable is the best tool of all for this (Figure 12-16). Both the inside and the outside tip of the burnisher are used to press the top of the bezel closer to the stone (Figure 12-17 and 12-18).

As a final step, run the edge of the burnisher around the upper edge of the bezel, pushing down on it (Figure 12-19). This will smooth out any rough spots you may have created during bezeling.

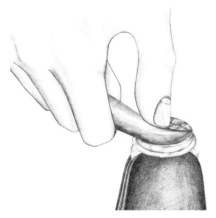

Figure 12–18. Setting the stone: the inside edge of the burnisher can also be used to press the bezel top closer to the stone.

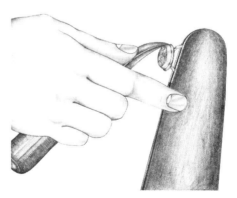

Figure 12–19. Setting the stone: smooth out rough spots by running the edge of the burnisher around the upper edge of the bezel.

ADDITIONAL TECHNIQUES

1) Decorative Bezels

A simple bezel can be embellished just using a saw, a drill, and various needle files (Figure 12-20). If you are using a fine silver bezel, this can be done most easily once it has been braced by being soldered to the base. Half-round beaded wire or twisted wire can also be soldered around the bezel to create an interesting decorative effect.

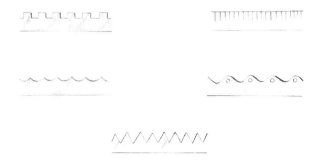

Figure 12–20.   Embellishing a simple bezel.

2) De-Bezeling

If you for some reason have to remove a stone from a setting without damaging the bezel itself, good luck! If you are very careful, maybe you can do it. The main problem will be getting something in between the stone and the inside of the bezel. You can try inserting the very tip of the burnisher or a pointed nailfile. Then, after running it along the inside edge a little, try prying it free of the stone, using the tool as a lever. This must be done very gradually, going around the stone quite a few times before it will begin to come free.

3) Inlay

Another method of setting turquoise, one which stretches back to nearly the dawn of the craft, is the technique of inlay. The contemporary masters of "mosaic-style" inlay are the Zuni Indians, who according to tribal history learned it in the late nineteenth century from a Navajo man named Atsidi Chon (Ugly Silversmith). The work is remarkably reminiscent of turquoise inlay work done by Late Dynasty Egyptian craftsmen. Stones are first cut to fit into channels which make up an overall design, then (these days) glued in with jeweler's epoxy (although the early Zuni craftsmen used piñion tree pitch as an adhesive). In sad point of fact, however, much "Zuni" inlay work on the market these days is set with nothing more than coral- or turquoise-colored cement.

A second method, "chip" inlay, is somewhat more random. Rather than being individually fitted, the pieces are laid into the pattern until the area has been covered. This technique will be discussed in Projects 9 and 10.

4) *Bezeling on Curves*

If you wish to solder a bezel to a curved surface, it will be necessary to curve the bottom of the bezel to obtain a close fit. Use a large half-round file to get the basic curve (Figure 12-21), then refine it with a half-round needle file until the bezel sits flush. Have patience—this may take some time. In addition, a piece of wire or strip of sheet will have to be soldered

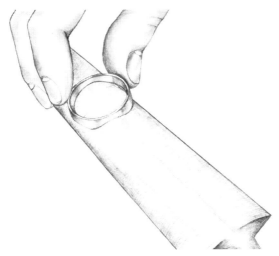

Figure 12–21. To solder a bezel to a curved surface, you must curve the bottom of the bezel with a half-round file.

to the inside edge of the bezel to allow the stone to rest level (special jeweler's sawdust or even ordinary sawdust can be used to do the same thing). You can also purchase "step-bezel" (bezel wire with a ready-made inner ledge) at the jewelry supply shop.

CHAPTER 13

Shaping Wire, Rings, and Bracelets

"The hand thinks and follows the thoughts of the material."
Constantin Brancusi

"You will also need by you two pairs of stout little pliers."
Benvenuto Cellini

Silver is an elastic metal. Correctly handled, it can be stretched, pounded, curved, bent, and twisted into almost any conceivable shape. Throughout history it has been prized for its unique ability to give life, substance, and dimension to the invisible world of the craftsman's imaginings.

Skillful use of crude shaping tools on precious metals produced some of the most impressive artifacts of the ancient world. The beaten metal ornaments of the Inca are regarded with almost superstitious awe by the craftsmen of today. Yet they were accomplished exclusively with tools harking back literally to the Stone Age. As one astonished Spanish contemporary wrote of those Peruvian goldsmiths,

> . . . they knew not how to make an anvil, whether of iron or anything else . . . neither could they make hammers . . . they used certain very hard stones, of a color between green and yellow . . . these they flattened and smoothed one against the other, and held them in great estimation.

Though the tools have changed somewhat, the principles are identical. It is still a matter of pounding the silver on a hard surface or bending it

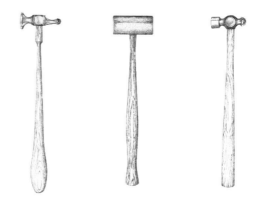

Chasing hammer   Rawhide mallet   Ball peen hammer

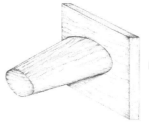

Homemade bracelet mandrel

Modified baseball bat

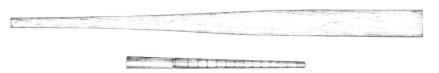

Ring mandrel

Round-nose pliers   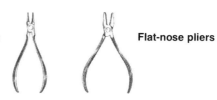   Flat-nose pliers

Figure 13–1.   Tools for shaping.

around a particular shape. And craftsmen of today are no less adept at using improvised tools to coax metal into following the outlines of their creative vision.

For simple bending and shaping of silver, you will need only a few very basic tools. If you develop an interest in the process you will undoubtedly start collecting more.

TOOLS

Jewelers' pliers are used to shape small pieces of sheet and wire. A basic toolbox should include two pairs: a round-nose and a flat-nose type. You will find them invaluable when your hands just aren't equal to the task of directly shaping the metal. Each one has a specialized function. Flat-nose pliers are used for flattening small pieces, aligning edges, and making sharp, right-angle bends in the metal. Round-nose pliers are used primarily for bending curves. Make sure when purchasing pliers that the inside of the jaws is absolutely smooth.

The most versatile tool of all is the human hand, and wherever possible you should use it.

Hammers in jewelrymaking are used in the same way hammers always are: for hitting things. The rawhide hammer is used to form the silver to whatever it is being pounded against without flattening, stretching, or otherwise distorting the surface. It is also used to make small ring and bezel enlargements; being relatively soft, it will do the job without making dents.

The ball peen hammer and the French chasing hammer (or open flat-faced hammer) are used to actually spread metal out. The chasing hammer, having a large flat face, tends to make fewer marks on the silver, and is particularly good for forging against curved surfaces. The ball peen, which has a smaller, slightly convex face, is more effective on flat surfaces. As a first tool, the ball peen is probably the more versatile. A 12-ounce Dixon #27 is good, or you can make your own by sanding down and then buffing an ordinary machinist's ball peen. The main consideration is that the face of the hammer be free of scratches and indentations. After hammering, tool marks can be removed by filing or left as they are for decorative effect.

Mandrels are graduated solid forms used in making and measuring bracelets, finger rings, outside bordering rings, etc. There are several varieties. The ring mandrel, one of the most standard of jeweler's tools, is used for measuring and forming rings. It consists of a tapered cylinder of solid steel, cut with markings which represent standard ring sizes. Bracelet mandrels are a similar tool, shaped in a rough approximation of the human wrist. The fashioning of bracelet and other home-made mandrels will be discussed later in the chapter.

A bench block of some sort is a handy workshop addition. It is used as a surface on which to flatten silver. Because the solid steel blocks sold in jewelers' supply shops tend to be rather expensive, craftsmen often improvise their own. Any flat, smooth, metal surface will do: an upended flatiron or household iron supported on a stand, an old iron hot plate, a piece of scrap metal, etc., Indian craftsmen often used sections of railroad ties. Machine shops are a good place to search. They often have scraps of leftover steel plate they will let you have or purchase for a nominal price.

TECHNIQUES

Although silver is noted for its ease of forming, still, as blues singer Sippie White once said, "You got to know how." Silver is not Silly Putty. After a certain point its "give" will start to give out. It will become harder and harder to bend, and can actually become brittle enough to crack.

This gradual stiffening of the metal—the result of compression and subsequent distortion of its molecular structure—can be relieved by a process called *annealing*. In heating the metal to a dull red color and then quenching it in pickle, the molecules spread out and resume their original positions, transforming the silver once again into a malleable and accommodating metal.

Silver is annealed as a matter of course prior to any bending or forming operations. Whether to anneal again is determined by using a special tool—the human hand. As you become familiar with the feel of the metal, you will sense the strain in the metal as readily as you perceive a tight muscle in your own back. When the metal passes the line between springy and rigid, don't try to force it. Annealing really doesn't take much time in relation to the trouble it can save you.

Although a charcoal block is a perfectly adequate annealing surface, a Chinese wok-type cooking pan filled with charcoal or pumice chips can make certain types of jobs, especially those involving bigger pieces, a lot easier. If set on a heat-resistant surface, the pan can be rotated on its rounded bottom to give the torch easier access to all parts.

BENDING WIRE

There is vast disagreement among jewelry historians over the methods used by early craftsmen to make wire. Suggestions concerning technique have ranged from the rolling of metal strips between two flat rocks to the use of drawplates not much different from the modern variety. However they did it, the delight that ancient Persian, Greek, and Egyptian craftsmen found in making decorative wire is evident in the work they left behind.

Throughout history, the most universally favored wire design motif has been the curlicue or "scroll." The basic method of making this ancient design is as follows:

1. Anneal a length of wire, 16 gauge or thinner (this can be snipped with ordinary wire cutters or cut with a saw).

2. Grip the end of the wire with the very tip of the round-nose pliers. Using the thumb of the free hand, press the wire tightly around one of the round jaws until you have formed a little circle (Figure 13-2A).

3. Rotate the pliers gradually, using the free hand to maintain tension in the wire (Figure 13-2B).

4. Continue twisting until you get a basic curlicue. The index finger is placed on the wire to guide it as well as to guard against kinks (Figure 13-2C).

When you are using the pliers, the third finger or pinky of the pliers hand should be braced against the handle to control the pressure exerted by the jaws on the metal.

TWISTED WIRE

Twisted wire can give an element of design interest to even the simplest setting. After being soldered along its length, the piece of twisted wire can be flattened and made into a ring, used to adorn a bezel, curved into a bracelet, ad infinitum. By combining different gauges, thicknesses, and shapes of wire, a vast palette of simple embellishments can be created.

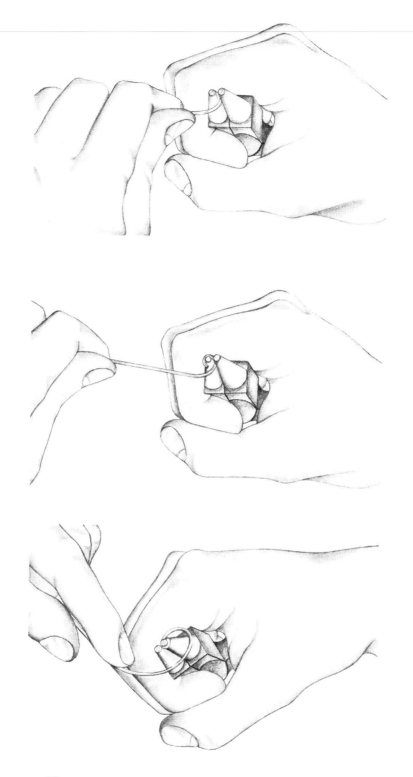

Figure 13–2. Bending wire with round-nose pliers.

Wire is generally twisted into a strand using one of two methods. In the first one, a length of wire is first bent in half and its free ends clamped into a vise. It is then twisted from the loop end using a hand drill whose end has been fitted with a hook or a bent nail (Figures 13-3, 13-4). Altnernatively, a large nail can be inserted through the loop and the wire twisted by hand. In this latter method, some craftsmen thread the loop through an empty spool to keep kinks from developing.

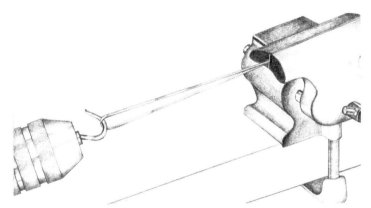

Figure 13–3. Twisting wire: clamp the ends of the loop in a vise.

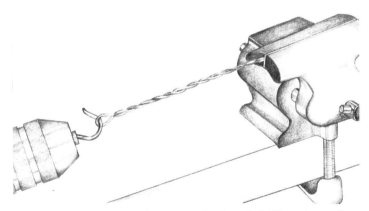

Figure 13–4. Twisting wire: turn the hand drill to form the strand.

FLATTENING WIRE

Flattening out all or part of a round wire design with a hammer can add interesting shapes and contours to your piece. It is also an elementary introduction to the process of forging. After annealing, the wire is flattened against the bench block with the ball peen or the chasing hammer. If the top of a ring is to be forged out, it is done on the ring mandrel. During any kind of forging, hammer blows should overlap so that the metal will flatten smoothly. You should try to spread out the metal much like a piece of dough, working it evenly in the general direction you want it to go.

Tool marks left by the hammer are an unavoidable byproduct of forging. These can be filed and sanded away, or left for textural interest.

MAKING RINGS AND RING SHANKS

The shank is that part of the ring which goes around the finger. Since the day some anonymous Sumerian first thought it up, ring shanks have shouldered weapons, love tokens, signets, diamonds, and glass. At the same time, due to the rather consistent shape of the human finger, the shanks themselves have undergone little change. There are two types of shank (Figure 13-5). One is a continuous circlet of wire or sheet, with the

Figure 13–5. The ends of the shank can either meet in a continuous circle or be soldered separately to the platform.

stone mounted either on a platform or directly on the curve of the shank. The other, referred to as a split shank, has each end soldered separately to the platform. Besides bringing the face of the ring closer to the finger, the split shank is somewhat easier for the beginner to construct.

The easiest way to measure how much metal you will need for a ring shank is to wrap a strip of construction paper tightly around the knuckle of the finger in question, mark the overlap, and measure the length. To this add a length equal to three times the width of the metal you are using (which compensates for the compression of the ring's inner surface when it is bent in a curve), and cut the silver to size. With the split shank, you will have to subtract a little of the gap between the ends of the shank (usually ⅛ to ⅜ inch). Alternatively, you can measure the wire by wrapping it around the mandrel at the appropriate place, then cutting it to size.

To form the split shank into the proper shape, you may either: 1) bend it into a U-shape over the mandrel using your fingers, then hammer the ends down over the mandrel with the rawhide mallet, or 2) after hand-bending, roll the shank between the mandrel and some hard surface (the edge or the surface of the work table) until the ends have been properly curved. Check the fit before soldering (Figure 13-6). Remember, at this

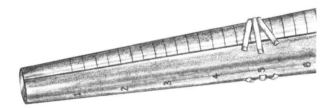

Figure 13–6. After shaping the split shank, check its size on a calibrated ring mandrel.

point, you can still bend the feet closer together or further apart to change the size. Before soldering, bevel the "feet" flat with a file and then sand them so they make a close join with the platform. (See Figure 13-7 for examples of split shank patterns.)

In the case of round shanks, the length of the ring blank can either be obtained from a ring size/ring blank conversion table, computed mathematically, or measured with construction paper. In the second method, the formula used is Length = (inside diameter + metal thickness) × 3.14. To form the solid shank, use the following procedure:

1. Cut the wire or sheet to the right size and file the edges even (10 to 14 gauge wire or 16 to 20 gauge sheet are the most commonly used widths).

2. After annealing the metal, use fingers, jeweler's pliers, rawhide mallet, or any combination thereof to bend the ring blank until the ends meet.

Don't worry if it is not round at this point; it will be trued up later.

3. Press the ends past each other until enough spring is built up to hold them flush. This is the same technique which was used in constructing a bezel, but in this case you may have to use pliers to create the necessary tension.

4. Solder the join with hard solder, pickle, and file away the solder seam.

5. Form the ring into a perfect circle on the mandrel, hammering it with the rawhide mallet. Then slide it off and true it in the reverse direction (Figure 13-8) to compensate for the tapering effect of the mandrel.

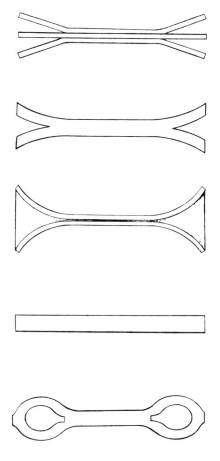

Figure 13–7. Some suggestions for split shank patterns.

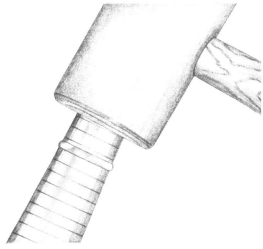

Figure 13–8. The ring must be trued in the opposite direction to compensate for the tapering of the mandrel. Slip it off, turn it around, and hammer again around the appropriate marking.

If the shank is to be soldered to a platform, it is first filed flat at the top. If a bezel is to be fitted directly on top of the band, file the bottom of the bezel into a curve (see Figure 12-21).

FORMING LARGE RINGS

Sometimes you may wish to make a large diameter ring of round, half-round, or twisted wire to use as a border around a flat circle (see Project 10) or as a frame for a free-standing design (Project 8). In the spirit of both the great tradition of tool improvisation *and* the Great American Pastime, we recommend that you go out and purchase a baseball bat; after sawing off the handle and the end, you will have the best large ring mandrel there is. You can even calibrate it, inserting it through the various holes in your circle template and marking the various diameters with a scriber or a felt-tip pen. The markings will enable you to measure the length of wire for a given circle by wrapping it around the bat at an appropriate point. After soldering, the ring is trued (or enlarged if necessary) by hammering it around the wood at the appropriate marking.

BRACELET FORMING

If you make your bracelet out of half-round 8 gauge wire, you can bend it by hand without much trouble, providing you have annealed it properly first. Measure the wrist with construction paper, leaving a gap approximating the width of the wrists between the ends so that the bracelet can be turned sideways and slid onto the arm. However, when a design calls for a heavier gauge of wire or sheet, most professional jewelers generally use a steel mandrel to shape the silver. However, these are usually quite expensive (thirty dollars or more) and as a result many hobbyists devise alternative tools and methods. A partial list of the tools we have seen used includes rolling pins, table legs, old auto tailpipes, railway ties, broom and rake handles, even a section of hard plastic irrigation hose. In fact, any object which contains the two or three basic curves that comprise a bracelet shape can be used to gradually bend the metal into the right shape.

However, the best mandrel substitute for the money is one made from the last five inches or so of a pick axe handle (Figure 13-1, Homemade Bracelet Mandrel). The handles are available at most good hardware stores for about five dollars, and, when mounted in a horizontal position on the side of the work surface, they will serve you just as well as a commercial bracelet mandrel.

There are three possible approaches to making a bezeled bracelet. One is to bend the bracelet first and then solder the bezel to it, which involves either filing the top of the bracelet flat so the bezel will sit level, or filing the bottom of the bezel to fit the curve. Another method is to solder on the bezel first and bend the bracelet afterwards. There are two risks with this method: one, you may accidently mash the bezel with a hammer as you are shaping the bracelet; secondly, the bezel may be pulled out of shape anyway by the curving of the backing metal. If you are using a narrow oval stone with either of these, most of the problems will be negligible. If not, you will just have to "futz", keep adjusting until you get everything to fit. A third possibility is to construct a platform and shank style bracelet in basically the same way as you would make a platform ring (See Project 11).

The correct procedure for forming a bracelet on a mandrel is as follows:

1. After annealing the sheet or wire, center it on the mandrel and bend down the ends by hand (Figure 13-9A).

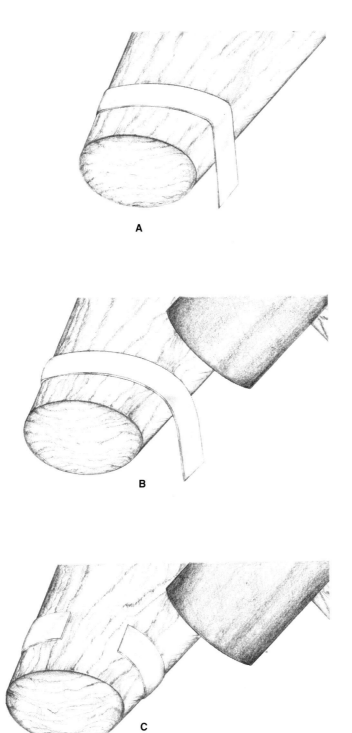

Figure 13–9.   Forming a bracelet on a mandrel: bend down the ends, hammer the metal against the curve, and pound down the ends.

2. Using the rawhide mallet, hammer the bracelet against the curve of the mandrel, starting with the "shoulder" (Figure 13-9B).

3. Turn the bracelet over and pound the ends down on the mandrel (Figure 13-9C).

The shaping should be done in a symmetrical manner. Work on one side for a while, then the other, then back again. It's like a married couple sharing a blanket. If one pulls some of it over too much to one side, the other will have to pull it back, until some kind of equitable distribution has been reached.

In general, remember that shaping is a gradual process. Do it bit by bit, section by section. If you respect the metal, you will be able to work with it. If you try to force it, to bend it to your will, the force will bounce back on you.

CHAPTER 14

Finding and Chain

"Certain foolish young men have lately brought about a new fashion. They have begun to fasten their shoes and knee-bands with buckles instead of ribbons, wherewith their forefathers were content and moreover found them more convenient. Surely every man will own that they were more decent and modest than these new-fangled, unseemly clasps or buckles, as they will call them, which will gall and vex the bones of these vain cox-combs beyond sufferance and make them repent of their folly. . . . It belongeth to the reverend clergy to tell these thoughtless youths, in solemn manner, that such things are forbidden by Scripture."

Editorial in Seventeenth Century
English Newspaper

Jewelry wouldn't be jewelry unless there was some way to attach it to the body. It would be a beautiful possession, certainly, like a silver tea service or a fine painting. But worn on the body, jewelry transcends the limits of the merely *owned:* it is an expression of the being, an intimate companion in the affairs of daily life. We may try to deny it, but there is an indefinable glow, an almost magical feeling of investiture, when you first put on something you have made.

It is a testimonial to man's ingenuity that so many different ways have been devised to wear jewelry. Although many of these originated as a means of fastening a garment, the inexhaustible human concern for embellishment has led, at one time or another, to gems being worn from the crown of the head to the tips of the toes and all points in between.

The fashion of the day has see-sawed from one extreme to the other throughout recorded history. Personal jewelry nearly disappeared in England and France during the eleventh and twelfth centuries. This was due not only to a general impoverishment of the realm but to the clothing of the time; long-sleeved, high-necked tunics allowed little space for personal decoration.

In other times and especially in the case of the crowned heads of state, jewelry was affixed to every available part of the person, even to the point of being sewed into the clothing. This often increased the weight of the traditional burdens of office to nearly unbearable proportions, as can be seen from the following description by a European traveler of a ruling Indian maharani in full dress:

> The weight of her jewels was so great that she could not stand without the support of two attendants. Her anklets of gold, studded with emeralds, weighed over 100 oz. each . . . Over her slender feet she wore flat strips of gold attached by chains to jeweled toe rings. The same precious metal covered the backs of her hands and was held in place by diamond links attached to her rings and bracelets. She could not bend her elbows because her arms were covered solidly from wrist to shoulder with wide bracelets of precious stones. Diamonds blazed upon her breast and hung in a multitude of chains far below her waist. Her throat was stiffened by collars of emeralds and rubies.

Today's fashion, fortunately, makes simplicity, elegance, and comfort the prime determinants of how jewelry is to be worn. Above all, the various pins, catches, loops, and other fastenings (generally referred to as "findings") must be practical and functional. If something is to hang, it must hang straight. If it is to be pinned to the clothing, the pin must hold securely.

At the same time, there are aesthetic considerations. The finding or chain must be considered in the light of the piece itself. Often the most appropriate choice is the simplest. Other times, something a little more ornate adds that extra touch of design interest which makes the piece really work when it is worn.

There are a wide variety of commercial findings available through craft outlets. In many cases you will deem it much more sensible, as many jewelers do, to buy your findings and chains ready-made. On other occasions, you will wish to fashion your own, both for the satisfaction of making a piece in its entirety, and because there is nothing readily available which will be as suitable. Either way, a good working knowledge of the most commonly-used items and techniques is absolutely indispensable.

PENDANT AND NECKLACE FINDINGS

Jump rings have always been the findings most commonly used to attach a piece of jewelry to a chain. Simple gold loops adorn the most lavishly conceived Medieval and Renaissance neckwear. Although they are inexpensively available from jewelry supply shops in a wide variety of calibrated sizes, it is useful to know how to make your own.

The simplest way to do this is to wrap a length of 18 or 20 gauge wire around a nail or a thin wooden dowel, remove the coil, and saw it through. The saw is preferable to wire cutters, as it will produce even ends which can be soldered together without filing. Note that the saw is held at an angle (Figure 14-1), so that the link being cut through serves as a guide to start the next one. Rather than wrapping the wire by hand, some jewelers prefer to put the nail or a wooden dowel in the end of the drill with the end of the wire along side it, tighten down the chuck, and feed the wire onto the revolving spindle with the free hand.

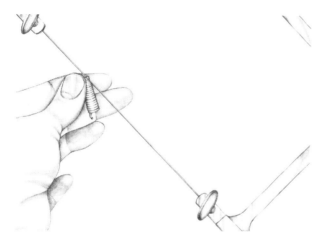

Figure 14–1. When cutting loops, angle the saw so each cut can guide the next.

Whether a piece of jewelry is to be a pendant or a necklace is determined largely by the length of its chain. In either case, the variety of findings is limitless. Inserting a jump ring through a hole drilled at the top of the piece and soldering the ends together is one kind of finding. Other common ones are made from hollow tubing or wire semicircles, or by bending a tongue of metal left at the top of the piece into a loop (Fig. 14-2).

Particularly in the case of pendants, the chain should be able to move easily through the finding. Otherwise, especially with long chains, the piece will not remain centered but will swing like a pendulum, creating a hazard for innocent bystanders.

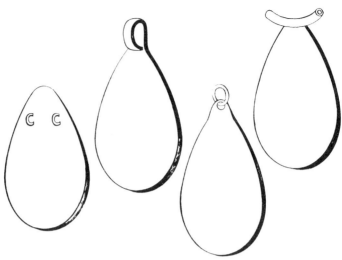

Figure 14–2. A chain can be strung through wire semicircles, a bent tongue, a jump ring, or hollow tubing.

BROOCHES

The fact that brooches have been worn in so many different positions at different periods in their history is as much attributable to changes in function as the shifting winds of fashion. Brooches originated as fastening pins, and were relied upon to keep everything from tunics to kilts from departing the realm of modesty.

As clothing became more sophisticated, style as opposed to function became the prime determinant of what form brooches took. Sometimes, as is often the case today, the "jet set" started new trends in wearing habits. For example, when Charles II married Catherine of Braganza, the large knot-shaped shoulder brooches common in her native Portugal became an instant fad among English fashion plates. In the sixteenth century, brooches were worn almost exclusively as hat badges called *enseignes*.

The modern brooch finding consists of three separate elements: a pin, a pin joint, and a catch (Figure 14-3). The joint and catch are soldered to the back of the piece, after which the pin is inserted into the joint and squeezed into place with the flat-nosed pliers. There are two important considerations in placing the findings: 1) both joint and catch must be above the median line of the piece if it is to hang properly; 2) the joint

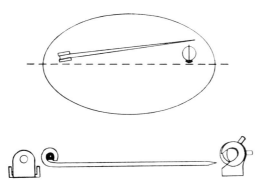

Figure 14–3. A brooch finding is composed of a pin joint, pin, and catch.

should be soldered at such an angle that the pin, when inserted in the catch, will be held there by tension as well as by the catch itself (Figure 14-3).

The findings are soldered by placing solder snippets around them or by premelting solder in place on the back of the brooch before setting them into position. Some jewelers like to add a brooch finding to a pendant to give the owner a choice of how it is to be worn on a given occasion.

EARRINGS

There are several different types of earring findings. Figure 14-4 illustrates the major ones currently in use: the screw back, clip-on, the post, and the ear wire. All but the ear wire must be soldered to the earring using

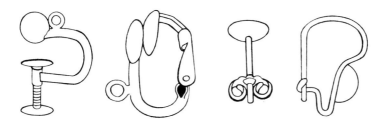

Figure 14–4. The major types of earring findings are (from left) the screw back, clip-on, post, and ear wire.

a soft, lead-based silver solder (Stay-Brite is the brand most commonly available). This should be done as follows:

1. Touch the spot, the finding, and the earring at their point of contact with a little liquid soft-solder flux (usually provided with the solder).

2. Melt a small piece of soft solder into the earring cup with a low flame (soft solder has a melting point of eight hundred degrees lower than easy solder). Allow it to cool, then place it into position.

3. Heat the entire piece gently until a thin line of solder shows around the cup, then allow it to cool. The cooling process can be hastened by dropping water from a fingertip onto the finding.

4. After it has hardened a little, drop it into cool water to completely solidify the join.

5. Clean the piece thoroughly, either by scrubbing with soap and pumice or boiling it in a solution of sodium bicarbonate. The flux is composed of glycerine and muriatic acid, and left-over traces can inflict painful burns on the ear lobes.

BELT BUCKLES

If you are one of those whose waistline goes through seasonal fluctuations, your belt-buckle will often find itself on the front lines of your own personal battle of the bulge. Belt buckle findings, therefore, should always be designed above all for strength.

There are several types of findings in general use (Figure 14-5), the most common being the buckle hitch (belt holder) and the peg combination. The peg is generally made from 8 or 10 gauge round or square wire. The hitch can be made from 16 gauge or thicker sheet silver or from the same gauge wire as the peg. Many craftsmen like to bevel the bottoms of the findings to give the join added strength by putting more surface area in contact with the base. This will also reduce the distance that the findings protrude from the base. Similarly designed commercial buckle backings with hinged buckle hitches are also available. A second type of belt buckle, fitted with a simple hinged pin, allows for additional design possibilities.

CHAINS

Making chains has always been an important part of the jeweler's art. In nearly every metal-working civilization save the Peruvian Chimu—

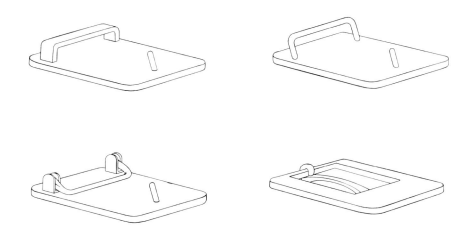

Figure 14–5. Buckle findings (from top right): square hitch and peg, round hitch and peg, hinged hitch and peg, and simple hinged pin.

who believed that repetition offended the gods—endless, shimmering strands of precious metal have exerted their strange fascination. Henry VII, one of history's most avid collectors, is said to have been fond of wearing a mammoth golden chain weighing over seven pounds.

Interestingly, chains also served as an early prototype of the checkbook. From ancient Arabia to Renaissance Europe, standardized links of gold or silver were acceptable legal tender. On those occasions where a frantic search of burnoose or doublet yielded no coinage, the customer could simply snip a few links off his neck chain to cover the purchase.

Chains are not as tedious to make as many people suppose. True, it takes time, but it is also rather enjoyable. It is that same atavistic pleasure office workers derive from stringing paperclips together. Why it is pleasant is a question best left to the students of human behavior. Just be warned; it can be addicting.

Chain links are fashioned in basically the same way as jump rings. Wire is wrapped around some sort of mandrel, then the coil is separated into individual links.

To make round chain links, clamp a dowel along with the end of a piece of wire (12 to 18 gauge is most common) securely in a vise (Figure 14-6). Wrap the wire tightly around the dowel, then remove the coil and either saw it through or snip the links individually with wire cutters.

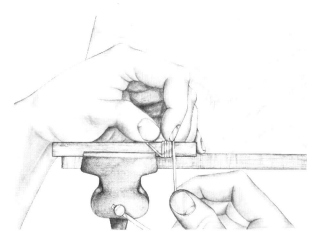

Figure 14–6.   When wrapping wire for round chain links, clamp the dowel and the end of the wire in a vise.

Most hardware stores carry assorted dowel kits which will give you a wide range of possible diameters.

A simple way to make an oval chain mandrel is by flattening out a length of thin-walled copper tubing. You may have to pound the wire lightly with a rawhide mallet once it is wrapped around the tubing in order to get it to lay flat. The links are cut or snipped at the narrow end for easy soldering.

Soldering chain links together one at a time can be a little tedious. The following is the most time-tested, time-saving sequence for fabricating chain: (Figure 14-7).

1. Solder two individual links closed.

2. Loop them back over an unsoldered link, then solder *that* link closed, forming a unit of three closed links.

3. When you have two units of three, attach them both to a seventh link.

4. Make another unit of seven and join it to the first one with a connecting link.

5. Keep going!

Once you have completed the chain, attach a clasp to the end links. Several simple home-made clasps are illustrated in Figure 14-8.

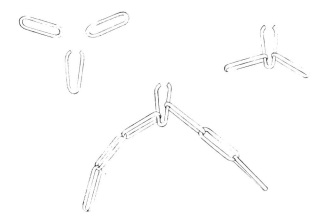

Figure 14–7. A time-saving sequence for soldering chain: solder two links closed, loop them over an unsoldered link, and attach two units of three links.

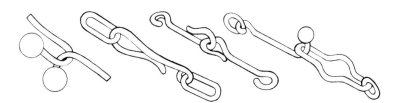

Figure 14–8. Finish your chain with a simple home-made clasp.

1) Loop-in-Loop Chain

Loop-in-loop chain is a design which has cropped up repeatedly in diverse historical locales. The ancient Romans were the acknowledged masters of this style. Their multi-loop construction method produced chain so fine that it resembled braided human hair. Italy's pre-eminence in the art of chain-making persists to this day.

The Moors and the Spanish after them made a much simpler version called the "money chain," so named because of the ease with which links could be removed and used for daily wheeling and dealing. These money-chains are made as follows (Figure 14-9).

1. Make a series of soldered oval links out of 18 gauge wire.

2. Bend them in half using round-nose pliers.

3. Join them together by slipping each link through the looped ends of the

one below it. When you have a chain of the desired length, solder a catch on the end links to prevent the chain from coming apart.

Figure 14–9.   Building a money-chain: bend oval links in half and join them by slipping each through the looped end of the one before.

VARIATIONS

An endless number of variations can be derived from a few basic shapes and techniques (Figure 14-10). Oval links can be squeezed in the middle with round-nose pliers (Figure 10D); the ends of bent loop-in-loop links can be pinched around a nail or a dowel and then flattened (Figure 10F); wire shapes can be soldered into the links or to each other (Figure 10G and H). A "dog-bone" chain can be made from partially flattened 8, 10, or 12 gauge wire lengths (Figure 10I); solid shapes can be joined with wire links (Figure 10J), to provide additional design possibilities.

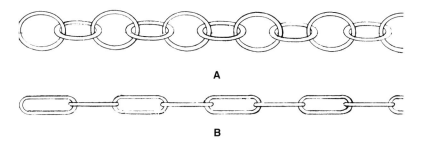

A

B

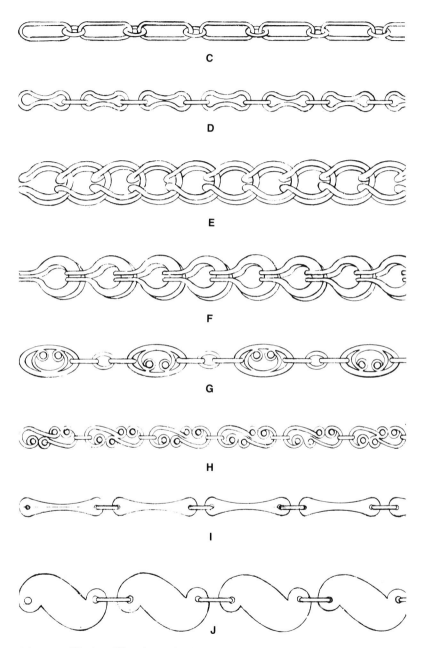

C

D

E

F

G

H

I

J

Figure 14–10. Chains like these look complicated, but they are derived from a few basic shapes and techniques.

CHAPTER 15

Finishing

"Give us the tools and we will finish the job"
Winston Churchill, 1941

Before it is buffed and polished, your project is still more a piece of *work* than a piece of *jewelry*. Although you can see what it will eventually look like, to your non-jewelry-making friends eyeing its dull sheen, tool marks, and scratches, it seems like something only a mother could love.

But finished, annointed with the almost unearthly glow of polished silver, it becomes something else entirely: a silent and luminous stranger, even in your eyes, looking like it was never "made" but somehow "brought forth" in one fell swoop of the imagination. The traces of its creation well covered, it finally stands on its own.

Finishing is essentially a process of fighting fire with fire. By using a series of graduated abrasives, one pattern of scratches is replaced by other yet finer scratches until the metal acquires its characteristic luminosity. Today, virtually all jewelers use machines to do final polishing. However, it is a good idea to have a working knowledge of the different techniques of hand-finishing, if for no other reason than to expand your options. Using a motor-driven polishing wheel to get at small areas of the piece is a little like using an elephant gun to hunt flies. In the long run, it is more time-consuming, as well as potentially more damaging, than using "appropriate technology" to get the job done.

Whichever way a piece is to be finished, however, there are several abrasives common to both methods:

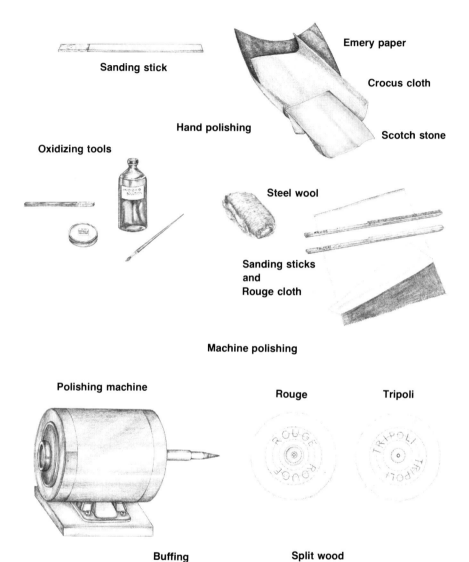

Figure 15–1.   Tools for finishing.

Emery paper is paper which has been coated with low grade corundum, the mineral which composes the gemstones ruby and sapphire. It comes in grades ranging from very fine to very coarse, (#1 through 3/0 being the ones most used by jewelers), and is used to remove solder stains, file marks, and other surface blemishes.

Tripoli, a silica-based buffing compound, is used to remove any small scratches still visible after using emery paper, as well as to create the smooth surface required for polishing. The silver is then given its final mirror-like sheen using any one of a number of special polishing compounds, the most common being a waxy red substance called jeweler's rouge. However, most craftsmen who work in turquoise and silver prefer a commercial compound marketed by the Dixon Company under the trade name "Zam Crocus." Light green in color and somewhat more powdery than rouge, it tends to leave less deposit on the piece, is easier to remove after polishing, and is less likely to cling to or penetrate the surface of the stone. If it does get into the cracks or matrix, its color makes it much less noticeable. Another commercial preparation, "Fabulustre," has similar advantages.

When using the various compounds, keep clearly in mind what each one is good for. Only tripoli is coarse enough to actually buff off scratches. Rouge and Zam are strictly "white collar workers." They will not do any heavy work. In fact, rather than eliminating scratches, the high shine they produce will only bring out any remaining surface blemishes all the more clearly.

HAND FINISHING

Finishing a few pieces by hand, although time-consuming, is a good way to become familiar with the surface properties of silver as well as with techniques which are useful adjuncts to machine buffing.

Emerying

Going over a piece with emery paper is the first step in both hand and machine finishing. To sand over a small area, tear a little off the sheet, fold it in half, and rub it briskly back and forth over the silver (if need be, you can wrap a strip around a needle file to get at the places more difficult to reach). When you have eliminated the large scratches or file marks with a heavier grade of paper, proceed to a finer grit, ending off with an iron-oxide-impregnated paper called crocus cloth.

If you have to cover a fairly large area, an emery stick is an almost indispensable aid. They are available commercially, but here is a way to make your own:

1. Take a flat or square wooden dowel and lay it over a sheet of emery paper. Make a line along the edge of the wood with a dull knife to help make a sharp crease (Figure 15-2). Continue folding the paper around the stick in this way until you have created two or three layers (Figure 15-3).

2. Staple the emery paper to the stick (Figure 15-4). You now have three separate working surfaces. When they become too worn to be useful, tear off the old layer to expose a fresh one.

Figure 15–2. Making an emery stick: first run a dull knife along the edge of the dowel to form a sharp crease.

Figure 15–3. Making an emery stock: wrap several layers of paper around the dowel.

Figure 15–4. Making an emery stick: staple.

Hand Buffing

Hand buffing and polishing are accomplished through the use of felt-covered sticks which have been charged with one of the appropriate compounds. They are transferred to the stick by first wetting the felt and then rubbing it over the compound. (If the buff is not moistened, the particles will not adhere.)

After the stick has dried, it is used by rubbing it briskly over the piece. A rouge cloth can be used for final polishing. Buffing and polishing compounds are removed from the piece by brushing it with soap and water using a soft toothbrush. Take care that all vestiges of tripoli have been cleaned off the piece before going on to any of the polishing compounds so as not to contaminate the rouge or Zam stick with coarser particles. Green soap, available from the drugstore, or household cleaners like Janitor-in-a-Drum are particularly effective.

Trumming

Trumming (or thrumming, take your pick), is a way to get into hard-to-reach places like the bottoms of bezels or the gaps between wires. A length of ordinary string or nylon cord is clamped into a vise and charged with buffing or polishing compound. The other end is then pulled taut and the string maneuvered into whichever areas of the piece need attention (Figure 15-5).

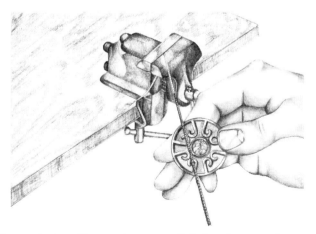

Figure 15–5.   Trumming to polish hard-to-reach spots.

Stoning

Scotch stones (also called Tam O'Shanter or Water of Ayr stones) are the equivalent of a very fine file or a medium coarse emery paper. They are often used to remove solder blemishes as well as to even out the surface of inlaid work. Scotch stones must always be used with water to avoid clogging them with silver or other particles. An ordinary facial pumice stone, available in drug stores, can be used in similar fashion. It is somewhat more abrasive, but very handy when larger areas have to be covered.

Steel Wool

Steel wool between 1 and 000 in coarseness can be used for pre-polishing or as a final step in the finishing process. Rubbing the piece with a little wad in *one direction only* produces a shiny matte texture known as a "scratch" or "butler" finish.

Oxidizing

Oxidation refers to the grey or black patina produced on the surface of the piece by using chemical solutions designed specifically for that purpose. This is done immediately before giving the piece its final polish—coarser compounds will only remove it. Although a lump of liver of sulphur dissolved in hot water will work quite well, commercial preparations such as Win-Ox, Hi-Lox, etc. tend to produce a darker finish and are more convenient. They are applied with a fine-pointed brush or a length of steel wire. Since they contain hydrochloric acid, they should be used with adequate ventilation.

A few hints:

1. Be sure to buff off the thin coating of fine silver left on the piece by the pickling process before applying the chemical, or the oxidation will not "take" as well.

2. Do not wash the piece with any solution containing ammonia; this will remove the patina.

3. A light application of vegetable oil will darken the color. Rub it off with a rag or paper towel afterwards so it doesn't collect dust.

4. If you wish to create highlights in the patina, use a wet toothbrush which has been dipped into some pumice powder to gently lighten the

oxidation where it seems appropriate.

5. Ordinary household bleaches such as Clorox will produce a light gray patina. A variety of other colors can be created using specific chemical solutions (see Appendix).

MACHINE FINISHING

Time being the commodity it is, you will probably want to eventually purchase a polishing motor. Not only does it do the work faster, but it is capable of creating a range of effects that are hard to obtain using only hand-finishing methods. However, keep in mind that a motor-driven wheel charged with buffing compounds is a mighty engine indeed. Like all powerful things, it has as much capacity for great harm as good. Therefore, a few friendly words of warning:

1. Be very careful about overbuffing your piece. The attractive blending of parts which occurs in machine polishing can easily become a blurring of the lines of the piece before you realize what is happening. Also, if you are not watchful, too much silver will be worn away, leaving your work with the look and feel of something from the bottom of a Crackerjack box.

2. Polishing wheels have sticky fingers. If you present your piece at the wrong angle, the wheel will snatch it out of your hand and hurl it against the nearest hard surface.

3. Machine polishing is messy. You should set up the motor a little distance from your work surface to avoid contaminating the area with polishing compounds. You should also either purchase a hood for the machine or make your own by cutting holes or curves in the side of a cardboard box and placing the machine inside it.

4. In general, flying particles of metal and polishing compound are not good for the eyes or lungs. Always wear safety goggles and a facemask when using the machine.

Buying a Polishing Motor

Commercial polishing motors are not only expensive (thirty-five to seventy-five dollars) but generally a little too fast for the average beginner. A good used 1725 or 1750 RPM motor—which will be just as effective for most jobs—can be picked up for a fraction of the price at a rummage sale, used tool shop, or appliance repair center.

Before purchasing a used motor, however, make certain that it is a single-speed type. Two-speed motors, such as the kind found in washing machines, have to be adapted. The best ones for jewelry polishing purposes come from clothes dryers, dishwashers, attic fans, home shops, etc., are rated between one-quarter and one-half horsepower, and will run on normal household current.

When you are shopping around for a used motor, be especially careful about "lemons." Sad to say, some people jump at the opportunity to foist their old burned-out machines on the unwary. Often these have frayed electrical cords, which are easily replaced if the rest of the motor is sound but make a "test drive" impossible. In general, if you can't start it, don't buy it. But in no case should you settle for bland assurances from the seller. Look for cracked or discolored casings indicating previous overheating. Check for a lingering burned smell near the shaft. Also, try turning the shaft by hand—it should move smoothly, without much back and forth play.

Once you have purchased your machine, you can have a tapered spindle (to hold the polishing wheels) fitted to the shaft at a lapidary shop. Since some motors rotate clockwise and others counterclockwise, you will have to get a spindle with appropriate threads (they come in right-handed and left-handed varieties). Tell the salesperson what you will be using it for and he will fit your machine with the one you need.

The motor should be bolted to a sturdy table, first making sure that the direction of rotation is *downwards* as you are facing it. If you don't have a separate polishing area, the motor can be attached to a ⅜ inch plywood platform with four rubber feet on the bottom to cushion the vibration. The entire unit can be moved aside when not in use.

General Method

To start off you will need two wheels, one for tripoli and one for polishing compound. Although fancier ones are available, muslin wheels, 6 or 11 inches in diameter, will be perfectly adequate. The very first thing you should do is *label them*. If you put tripoli on the rouge or Zam wheel by mistake you will have to discard it, or else you will wonder why the piece won't polish up while you are buffing half of it away.

The wheels should be screwed onto the spindle against the direction of rotation. They are charged by turning the motor and holding the compound against the revolving wheel for a few seconds (Figure 15-6). Let the wheel spin for a minute to discard excess particles. Figure 15-7 shows

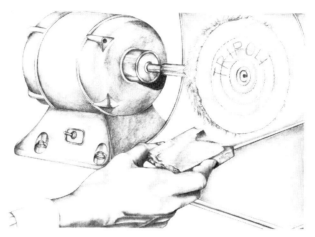

Figure 15–6. Charge the revolving wheel by holding buffing compound against it.

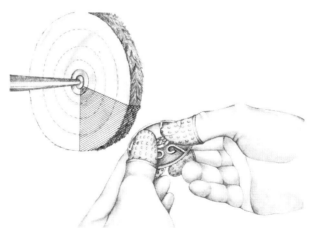

Figure 15–7. Buffing techniques: keep your fingers under the piece and use the shaded area of the wheel.

the proper way to hold the piece. Keep your fingers under it and hang onto it lest it be snatched untimely from your grasp. The shaded area indicates the part of the wheel which should be used in buffing operations.

When polishing chain, wrap it securely around a wooden dowel or similar object so that it doesn't wind up wrapped around the wheel. In general, it is safer to polish chain by hand. Extreme care must be observed when you are polishing anything with projecting edges that could be suddenly caught by the revolving buff. A pair of rubber fingertips, which can be purchased at an office supply store, will help you grip your piece, as well as to insulate skin from the heat of friction.

However, *don't let the piece get too hot,* or you will run the risk of discoloring your stone. Also, if you are using rouge and your turquoise has a lot of surface cracks or depressions, you may want to cover it with some masking tape to avoid getting the polishing compound imbedded where it will be difficult to remove. In general, avoid using too much abrasive or force if you want to keep the compounds from caking onto your piece.

You may at some point wish to purchase the following useful accessories for your machine:

1. An inside ring buff, which is used, as the name implies, for buffing the insides of rings.

2. A split wood emery paper ring lathe buff (try saying *that* fast ten times!). More commonly called a split wood buff, this versatile tool can be fitted with any grade emery paper or other abrasive paper you wish. A homemade emery buff can be made by rolling up a sheet of emery paper into a narrow tube, securing it with rubber bands, and sticking it on the polishing motor spindle (the spindle end will have to be wet down the first time so that it will fit snugly (1).

3. An eleven-inch, lead-centered soft muslin buff is a finer polishing wheel, and will tend to produce a slightly more lustrous final finish than the coarser variety. The larger circumference will increase the surface speed of the wheel.

When you are finished polishing your piece—or when you *think* you are—wash it in soapy water, using a soft bristle brush (or ordinary toothbrush) to remove the last traces of polishing compound. Rinse it off, then dip it in denatured alcohol and allow it to dry (this will help to eliminate water spots). Give it a quick once-over with a rouge cloth, or a piece of chamois, then take it outside and have a look at it. Normal daylight is the best light in which to look for flaws or scratches in silver.

If you are satisfied, congratulations. You are finished with finishing. If not, go back and finish some more. If at any point you find that a stubborn blemish has resisted your best efforts, go back to the previous stage, a coarser abrasive, rather than wasting your time and energy trying to accomplish something the process just isn't intended to do. This way you will be doing your part in conserving a very important form of energy: your own.

There does come a time in the life of every piece, though, when it has to be sent out into the wide world to fend for itself, a moment some jewelers find only slightly less traumatic than the last scene in "Love Story." If you are finding it hard to relinquish your piece, the words of philosopher Paul Valery may prove a good tonic. "An artist," he observed, "never really finishes his work; he merely abandons it."

CHAPTER 16

The Jeweler's Workshop

"Do what you can, with what you have, where you are."
                                    Teddy Roosevelt

In Theophilus' instructions on the building of a workshop, written about A.D. 1100, he called for a "high spacious building whose length extends to the east. . . ." For your workshop, a monster building heading east won't be necessary. What Theophilus was interested in getting across was the *concept* of a workshop. It is more than a place to work, it is a location of the spirit of the owner and a location of the spirit of any project.

Your workshop can be located anyplace in the house, and a good number of shops have been put up in attics, basements, outside garages and, at least once, a converted outdoor privy. The main point is personal preference. Some people seem to be able to work under any kind of noise conditions and some can't. And there are those who can work in extremely cramped spaces and those who cannot. It all depends on you. At least with jewelry making, there is little outside noise factor to be considered. It isn't a loud hobby, compared with amateur auto body work, blacksmithing, or taking up the study of African drum sounds. If it weren't for machine grinding and polishing on stones and jewelry pieces, the workshop could be located in any room in the house.

It might be wise, however, to use a separate room or a corner of the basement for the heavy work and the messy procedures. Machine grind-

139

Figure 16–1.   A Jeweler.

ing and polishing is slightly noisy and there is considerable residue that can get in and about furniture, drapes, and on carpets. Soldering is not the most friendly gesture to those living with you, either. Hot metal makes a very distinctive mark when dropped on carpeting and wood or tile floors.

The workshop should have adequate electrical outlets without stringing extension cords all over the room. The electric motor for machine polishing work should have a grounded plug and be in a grounded socket in the interests of safety.

Lighting in a workshop should be more than just the bare necessities. There should be overhead lights for some parts of the room and bright lights over the workbench. If possible, a workbench light should make more than one kind of illumination for different types of work. A large plastic magnifying glass (usually available in hobby stores or hardware places) is a good investment and quite handy for checking small jewelry pieces and small stones. It takes a little getting used to, with the magnifying glass, and it is sometimes hard to work under one, but the rewards in carefully finished pieces are worth the extra effort.

No one wants to imagine it, or prepare for it, but fires in workshops do happen, especially where torches and electrical devices stay. A first-class fire extinguisher handy to the workbench is a must. It doesn't cost much for the peace of mind.

Jeweler's workbenches have been made from almost every conceivable substance and in so many different ways that there is no standard. The stump (a real one or a good substitute) is a nice accessory for a workshop. A stump is a traditional item, probably adapted or borrowed from the Indian jewelers for whom it served as a bench, dapping block, tool holder, and anything else they could think of.

The usual workbench suffers from a peculiar trait; it is often too high in comparison to other benches and desks. This is good for hand and eye coordination—a must in jewelry making—but tiring on the arms, because the elbows have to be raised high to clear the workbench top.

A variation on the workbench is to make a "step" on the workbench, where the arms rest in a more level position and the hands, working on a raised step, are higher. With a swing-away magnifier, this could solve the fatigue problems associated with other benches.

It has been said too often that a clean workplace is a sign of little going on. That is not necessarily the case, and a reasonably orderly array of tools and places for them never hurt anyone. A sawblade and needle file rack can be made from a piece of cheap pine nailed or glued into an "L" shape. The shorter leg of the "L" is drilled for the various sized blades and files and then suspended from a wall above the workbench by nails or hooks on the longer part of the "L." A rack for pliers can be made the same way by drilling holes for one of the handles in the shorter "L" piece.

The quintessential peg board has graced thousands of shops and yours shouldn't be any exception; it's the cheapest and easiest way to get things up in their proper place and in an orderly fashion. If possible, put most of the tools on the wall above the workshop. Digging in drawers is a pain and drawers tend to collect more junk than tools. Save the drawers, if any, for scrap silver, notes, designs, and that sort of thing.

Somewhere in the workspace, put a well-stocked first-aid kit. It's good for the inevitable burns and scrapes that usually accompany jewelry making. A tetanus booster is another good idea. Most of us know what lockjaw is, but few of us have ever had it or know anyone who has. But it

Figure 16–2. Découpage à la scie.

does exist and there are plenty of ways to get it when using sharp tools around other pieces of metal.

Above all, your workshop is a private space. It's where a connection happens between you and something intensely personal—a piece of created, crafted jewelry. This is usually easy to see in another jeweler's workshop. Go in and pick up a tool, however innocently, at your own risk. Jewelers become almost pathological about their territorial space, mostly because there are so many little things lying about in an arrangement whose utility, if any, is known only to the craftsperson. No jeweler knows for sure what inspiration or future piece is lying around disguised as a piece of twisted scrap that anyone else would have thrown out.

And *use* the workshop. Too many people have a beautiful workshop and claim they "occasionally" do jewelry. A craft is a way to come into contact with an inner self, with art, if you will, in a metal and stone form. It can teach, astonish, reveal, and turn thoughts inward. It's good therapy and there's nothing wrong with the result, if you have fun doing craft work. In fact, there is quite a fine feeling when someone you know remarks on a piece of jewelry and asks where it came from. It means the piece was successful, apparently beautiful or unusual in some way, and you can say, in an off-hand way, ''I made it last week.''

CHAPTER 17

Introduction to the Projects

"We should appreciate what we are doing. There is no preparation for something else."

Suzuki Roshi, *Zen Mind, Beginner's Mind*

The projects in this section of the book are designed for the beginner. They advance in a gentle gradient, demonstrating the use of the different tools, techniques, and design concepts essential to making constructed jewelry.

By the time you do them all, you will know all you need to know about the basic methods of an ancient art. You will have explored everything we have been discussing first-hand. You will have made every major type of jewelry, from simple rings to bola ties. You will be familiar with a host of different design concepts, from contemporary Hopi-style overlay to the inlay techniques of the craftsmen of pre-Columbian Mexico. And, most importantly of all, you will have a nice collection of turquoise jewelry to show for your efforts.

Some of the projects call for calibrated stone, some for baroque cuts. Some can be traced directly off the page and followed by rote, others simply illustrate a particular method and leave you to adapt it to your own piece of turquoise. No matter what they are, the projects are intended as nothing more than training wheels, to be discarded once they have served their purpose.

And that purpose, essentially, is encouragement. You will not just be making "practice pieces." Whether you are presented with an adaptation of an outstanding design from the history of the craft or an original created to highlight a certain method, the end result will be something you will be proud to *wear.* By following a series of simple steps, you will arrive at a piece of jewelry that will be as valuable for what it *is* as for what it has taught you about how to make it.

No doubt you will make mistakes. The unforeseen will happen and you will have to improvise. But in the process you may well discover a way of doing things worlds better for you than the ones presented. The steps are only guidelines. They are not rules. In the final analysis, all that separates you from someone who has been at it for a decade is mistakes—he has made his, and learned from them; you have yet to make yours.

Don't be afraid to step out a little, to take a chance with your own inspiration. If you hit a snag, go back and refresh your memory on the basic principles and techniques and you will probably find a way around it. Making jewelry is an art, not assembly-line work. It requires a honing of the intuitive sense, a feeling for the uniqueness of each situation, each piece, and its potentiality for innovative solutions. You are in the same situation as a master carpenter. No matter how many times he has swung a hammer, he still has to watch what he is doing every time he hits the nail. And he will still come home from time to time with bruised thumbs, a reminder that in order to do anything well, even the most familiar gesture has to be approached as if for the first time.

A few practical notes, hints, and recommendations concerning the projects:

1. For the most part, the projects don't assume that you have done all the previous ones. You could, theoretically, start with the last one in the book and successfully perform all the operations simply on the basis of your previous reading. On the other hand, things are generally spelled out less as the projects proceed, on the assumption that after a while you will not want to be nagged about the basics. Therefore, it is recommended that you try to take them in sequence—the earlier projects are simpler, the steps are more explicit, and you will find that the sense of familiarity you gain with the tools and techniques will stand you in good stead as you proceed to the more complex pieces.

2. The patterns in the box at the top of each project are actual size—they can be traced directly off the page. However, unless your hand is quite steady, you will generally have to refine your initial copy somewhat before it is suitable for sawing. In the case of patterns which consist primarily of straight lines and regular curves (Project 10 for example), the following is a way of accurately transferring it from the book: first, lay the

tracing paper over the design and make dots at the important junctures of the lines. Then, connect the dots using a ruler and the appropriate templates. Besides being simpler, this method will involve fewer erasures.

3. Some of the projects suggest setting the piece you will be soldering on a few lengths of bent coat-hanger wire to enable you to direct the torch flame underneath the piece. In cases when delicate parts are being soldered on top of large pieces, most experienced jewelers devise some way of heating from the bottom. However, in the case of smaller projects (such as 3, 5 and 6), the wires have been recommended primarily to help you avoid the common beginner's mistake of melting the bezel while you are bringing the work up to soldering temperature. When you become more familiar with the torch and the heating process, using the technique is a matter of your own discretion.

4. With the exception of Project 5, you are left to your own devices as to what sort of chain or neck ring to use for necklaces and pendants. You may wish to make your own chains or simply, as most jewelers do, purchase one ready-made from the craft supply shop. In general, don't feel bound by the findings recommended in a given project. A pendant could, in many cases, just as easily be converted into a brooch or a necklace to suit your personal preference.

5. Generally speaking, the projects will require only those materials which are the most readily available. Even where a calibrated stone is called for, it will always be a fairly standard size. In addition, most of the pieces have been designed to allow a little leeway if you are unable to obtain a stone of exactly the size and shape illustrated. However, you may still occasionally find that you are unable to get hold of exactly what is specified. If this happens—to paraphrase the great '30s labor leader, Joe Hill—don't mourn, improvise. You can always enlarge, shrink, or otherwise alter a design to suit the stone you happen to have on hand at a particular moment. You should certainly exercise your own taste. If you are not entirely satisfied with the design which has been presented, change it—you may come up with something fairer in your eyes by far.

In general, no matter how much they are spelled out, the projects are not "TV dinners"—they can't be unthinkingly popped into the oven and come out the way they look on the label. *You* will have to provide the most important ingredients: care and patience, certainly, but also a little inspiration.

On the other hand, even though some of the projects involve quite a few separate steps, each individual procedure is basically quite simple. It is assumed that you have *read* the book but not that you have *memorized* it, so reminders and amplifications of previously covered material appear throughout the accompanying text.

Above all, relax and take your time. Although you may go about your work a little more slowly and hesitantly than the seasoned professional, in the end, you will come out with essentially the same result. And maybe even have a little fun to boot.

As you go along, keep in mind a remark which the Zen master Suzuki Roshi once made to his students: "In the beginner's mind, there are many possibilities, but in the expert's mind there are few. . . . This is also the real secret of the arts: always be a beginner."

Simple Pendant

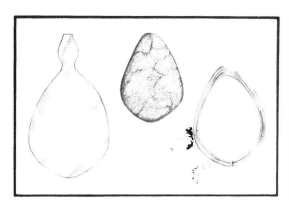

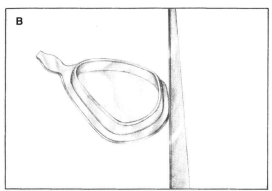

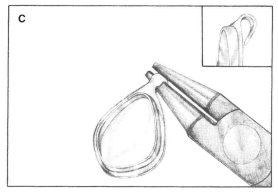

This simple pendant design can be used with any size or shape of stone, being essentially nothing more than a bezel cup with a surrounding "lip" of silver. It works particularly well with baroque cuts by attractively highlighting the natural assymetry of the stone.

MATERIALS

    (1) Turquoise cab (any shape)
    (1) Piece of bezel wire
    (1) Piece of 20 gauge silver sheet
       Medium and easy solder

TOOLS

Jeweler's saw with #1 blade
Propane torch
Needle file
Round-nose pliers
Curved burnisher and/or stone pusher

STEPS

1) Outline the stone on a piece of tracing paper, then draw a surrounding shape which follows the original at about ¼ inch distance all around. Draw a "tongue" at the top of the figure like the one shown in the pattern box.

2) Glue the tracing paper to the sheet of silver with rubber cement, allow a few minutes to dry, and saw out the design.

3) Measure the bezel wire to the stone, cut it to the proper length, and solder it together with medium solder as described in Chapter 12. Sand the bottom of the bezel and true it by re-inserting the stone.

4) Place the cut-out base on the charcoal block, flux thoroughly, and set the bezel in position. After allowing the flux to dry a little, place a sufficient number of solder snippets around the inside edge of the bezel using a flux-moistened brush.

5) Light the propane torch and heat the piece gradually up to soldering temperature with a moving flame (Box A). After the solder flows, play the flame briefly around the outside edge of the bezel to draw the solder into the seam, then pickle the piece in Sparex.

6) File around the edge of the piece with a needle file until the "lip" is uniform and even (Box B).

7) Using the round-nose pliers, roll back the tongue at the top of the piece to form the finding (Box C).

8) Bezel in the stone with the curved burnisher or a stone pusher.

9) Buff and polish the piece.

10) Fit with a commercial chain or make your own.

Overlay Pendant

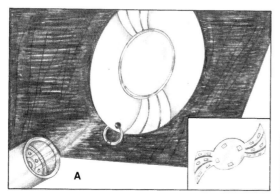

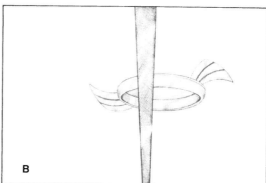

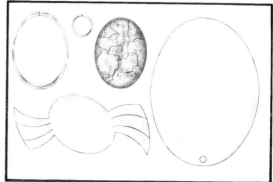

MATERIALS

(1) Turquoise oval, approximately 20mm x 15mm
(1) Piece bezel wire between 1⅝″ and 1¾″
(1) 1¾ inch by 2½ inch piece of 22-gauge silver sheet
(1) Jump ring
   Hard, medium and easy solder

TOOLS

Jeweler's saw with #1 blade
Hand drill with ¹/₃₂ inch drill bit

Propane torch
Needle file
Curved burnisher and/or stone pusher

STEPS

1) Saw out the patterns shown in the pattern box. Drill a hole in the oval base for the jump ring.

2) Measure the bezel, solder it together with hard solder.

3) Solder the bezel into place with medium solder (Box A).

4) File around the edge of the soldered bezel until the seam between it and the base piece is no longer visible (Box B).

5) File the ends of the jump ring even (if necessary), insert it through the hole in the base, and press-fit the ends so that they are held together by spring tension. Lay the base with the jump ring on the charcoal block, and flux it.

6) Flux the back of the overlay piece, place snippets of easy solder as shown in Box C (insert). Place one snippet of easy solder on the jump ring as shown. Allow the flux to dry. Then lay the top piece on the oval and heat the entire assembly with the propane torch until the solder flows. Quench the piece in pickle then rinse it in water.

7) Bezel the stone, then buff the piece.

8) Oxidize the cut-in lines of the overlay piece with oxidizing solution.

9) Polish.

Layered Ring

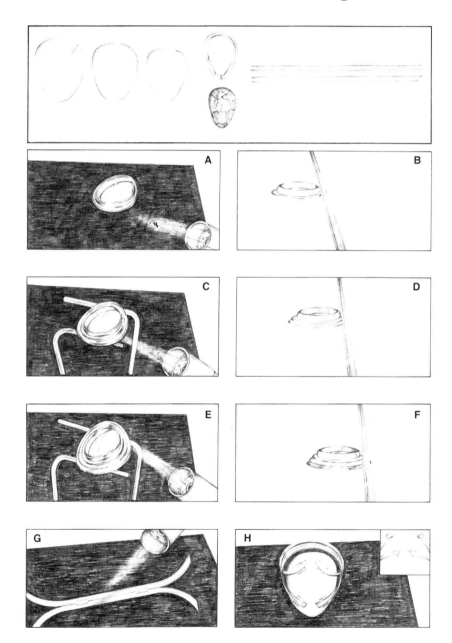

This is a good design to use with irregular shaped stones, although it works equally well with ovals or rounds. It is basically just a simple platform ring with built-up layers. You can leave the ring with one layer, creating a look similar to Project 1, or build it up to three layers as shown. Take your time filing between steps to insure even borders.

MATERIALS

(1) Turquoise cab (any shape)
(1) Piece of bezel wire
(1) Piece sheet silver, between 18 and 22 gauge, depending on the "heft" desired
10 gauge half-round wire
Hard, medium, and easy solder

TOOLS

Jeweler's saw with #1/0 or #1 blade
Propane torch
Bent coat-hanger wires
Needle file
Ring mandrel
Curved burnisher and/or stone pusher

STEPS

1) Trace around the outline of the stone, then draw a surrounding shape which follows the original at about ⅛ inch distance all around. Cut this out of silver.

2) Measure the bezel, solder it together with hard solder, and then solder it to the first piece with medium solder (Box A). Pickle the piece, then rinse it to remove any traces of Sparex.

3) File around the edge until you have an even "lip" which follows the shape of the stone (Box B).

4) Trace around the lip on a piece of tracing paper, then draw a

surrounding shape which follows the line about ⅛″ distance all around. Cut this out with a jeweler's saw.

5) Set the piece you have just sawed out on the charcoal block (if using 18 gauge silver or heavier, put a few lengths of bent coat-hanger wire underneath). Flux the surface. Next, place snippets of medium solder on the back of the already-soldered plate/bezel unit and set it on top of the piece on the block. Heat the whole assembly until the solder flows (Box C), then quench it in pickle and rinse it in water.

6) File around the edge until you have an even lip which follows the shape of the first plate (Box D).

7) Repeat steps 4 through 6 (Boxes E and F).

8) Determine what size shank you will need, then bend two pieces of 10 gauge half-round wire as shown in Box G. After sanding and then fluxing the points of contact, lay the wires side by side on the charcoal block. Apply a few snippets of medium solder with a flux-moistened brush and heat the wires until the solder flows. Pickle and rinse.

9) Bend the shank around a ring mandrel, then bevel the ends as shown in Box H (Insert), and clean them by rubbing them over #1 emery paper. Test to see that the shank will sit level. If one or more of the feet stick up in the air, bend them until all four sit flush on their bevelled ends.

10) Flux the back of the platform, set down the shank (make sure it is centered!), and wedge one good-sized snippet of easy solder behind each of the "heels" of the "feet" (Box H).

11) Heat the entire assembly until the solder flows, then pickle the piece.

12) Bezel in the stone, buff and polish (the inside ring buff is used to polish the inner diameter of the shank).

Simple Forged Ring

The graceful lines of this Scandinavian-style forged ring will accommodate a wide variety of different size and shape stones. The basic design can even be "doubled" for added effect. As a rule of thumb, the ring will be about 1½ sizes larger after it has been flattened with the hammer.

MATERIALS

(1) small turquoise cab (any shape)
   Bezel wire
   18 or 20 gauge sheet
   12 gauge round wire
   Medium and easy solder

TOOLS

Round-nose pliers
Ring mandrel
Propane torch
Rawhide mallet
Chasing or ball peen hammer
Locking tweezers
Curved burnisher and/or stone pusher
(Third hand)
(Carbon mandrel)

STEPS

1) Cut a length of 12 gauge wire, center it in the round-nose pliers (A) and bend it with your fingers (B).

2) Bend up the ends, leaving a loop in the middle (C).

3) Bend the wire over the mandrel (D).

4) After filing the ends of the wire even, press-fit them together and solder with medium solder. Pickle and rinse.

PROJECT 4–A. Center the wire in the round-nose pliers.

PROJECT 4–B. Bend the wire with your fingers.

PROJECT 4–C. Leave the loop in the middle, but bend up the ends.

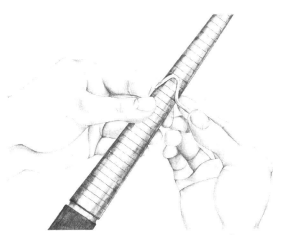

PROJECT 4–D. Bend the wire over the mandrel.

5) Hammer the ring into a curve on the mandrel, using the rawhide mallet (E).

6) Slip the ring over the mandrel and forge the original loop flat with glancing, overlapping blows from the ball peen or chasing hammer (F). Smooth away the hammer marks with a fine file.

7) Make a bezel cup (see Chapter 12), using hard-grade solder on the bezel and medium solder to join it to a piece of 18 or 20 gauge sheet.

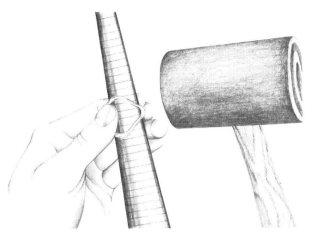

PROJECT 4–E.   Hammer the ring into a curve.

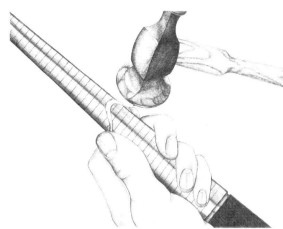

PROJECT 4–F.   Forge the original loop flat with glancing, overlapping blows from the ball peen or chasing hammer.

PROJECT 4–G.   With the flattened loop in contact with the base of the bezel cup, place easy solder snippets and heat the construction.

8) Place the bezel cup face down on the charcoal block. Clamp the ring in the locking tweezers, positioning them on a brick or other raised surface so that they hold the ring in the position shown in G (the "third hand" is particularly handy for this). Be sure that the flattened loop of the ring is in contact with the base of the bezel cup.

9) Place easy solder snippets as shown and heat the construction until the solder flows. Pickle and rinse. (G)

10) Bezel in the stone, using the curved burnisher and/or the stone pusher.

11) Buff and polish.

VARIATION

A double ring can be made using similar techniques, but you will need a carbon mandrel. The steps are as follows:

1) Make another ring in the same manner as the first.

2) Slide the two rings onto carbon mandrel and sit the bezel cup between them.

3) Twist the rings until you come up with a design you are satisfied with and which allows both rings to touch the base of the bezel cup.

4) Using a flux-moistened brush, place several snippets of easy solder as shown in H and Insert H, and allow the flux to dry them in place. Then heat the ring until the solder flows, playing the flame all around the ring. Pickle and rinse.

5) Bezel in the stone, buff and polish.

PROJECT 4–H. Placement of the solder snippets for the optional ring shank.

Eight-Petalled Lotus Necklace

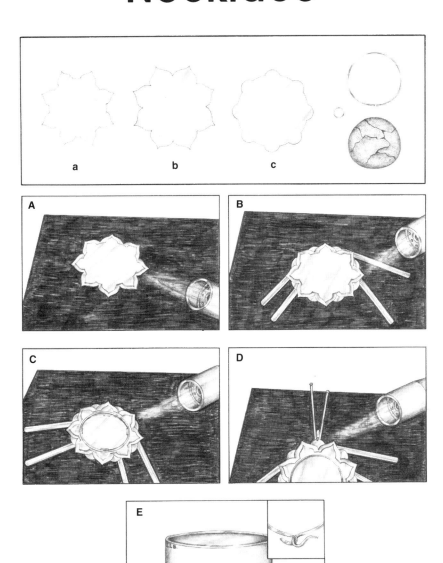

a   b   c

A

B

C

D

E

This is a further application of the layering method of construction. Floral designs work especially well, as the technique creates a distinctive "living" quality out of the flat pieces. The eight-petalled lotus is frequently seen in the religious art of the East. It symbolizes the qualities of compassion and generosity.

MATERIALS

(1) 18 or 19 mm turquoise round
(1) Piece of bezel wire, 1⅜ to 1½ inches long
(1) Jump ring
(1) piece of 22 gauge sheet silver, approximately 4 by 1½ inches
(1) Piece 12 gauge wire 1 - 1½ feet long
    Hard, medium, and easy solder

TOOLS

Jeweler's saw with #1/0 blade
Propane torch with medium tip
Bent coat-hanger wires
(2) Ordinary straight pins
Curved burnisher and/or stone pusher

STEPS

1) Use a saw fitted with a #1/0 blade to cut the three basic shapes shown in the pattern box. Try to be as accurate as you can—the symmetry of each piece is important to the overall look of the pendant.

2) Flux the smaller lotus (a), place some snippets of medium solder with a flux-moistened brush, and allow to dry. Set the larger lotus (b) on the charcoal block with the smaller one (a) solder side down on top of it and heat until the solder flows (Box A). Pickle and rinse.

3) Carefully file around the edge of the larger lotus with a needle file to make the outside line conform with the inner petals. However,

Project 1, Simple Pendant

Project 3, Layered Ring

Project 2, Overlay Pendant

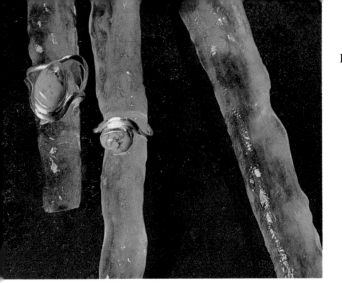

Project 4, Simple Forged Ring

Project 5, Eight-Petalled Lotus Necklace

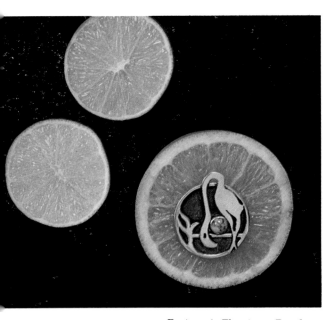

Project 6, Flamingo Pendant

Project 7, Wire Earrings

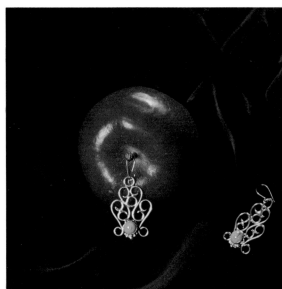

Project 8, Fish Pendant   Project 9, Inlaid Ring

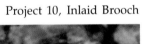

Project 10, Inlaid Brooch   Project 11, Flower Bracelet

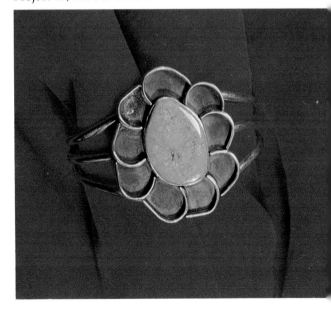

Project 12, Elk Bolo Tie

Project 13, Turquoise Maiden Buckle

Project 14, Hopi Indian Buckle

don't overdo this to the point where the outer petals become distorted.

4) Place the bottom piece (c) on the bent coat-hanger wires and flux it thoroughly. Place easy solder on the back of the previously soldered unit and lay it on top of the third piece. Heat, alternating the flame under and over the piece until the solder flows (Box B). Pickle and rinse.

5) Make the bezel, soldering it with medium solder. Place the previously soldered construction on the bent coathanger wires, flux the top and set the bezel into position. Place snippets of easy solder around the inside of the bezel and heat, alternating the flame over and under the piece until the solder flows (Box C). Pickle and rinse.

6) Solder the jump ring together with medium solder. File away the seam and sand a section of it clean. Also sand clean the edge of one of the "petals" of the lotus. Then place the jump ring upright between two straight pins which have been pushed into the charcoal block so that the sanded part of the ring comes into contact with the sanded part of the lotus petal. Flux the juncture, then place a snippet of easy solder and heat until the solder flows (Box D). Pickle and rinse.

7) Bezel in the stone, buff and polish the piece. A little extra buffing will help the pieces to "blend" into one another.

8) To make the neck ring, bend the ends of the 12 gauge wire as shown in Box E (Insert). It can then be shaped by wrapping it around a 1 pound coffee can.

Flamingo Pendant

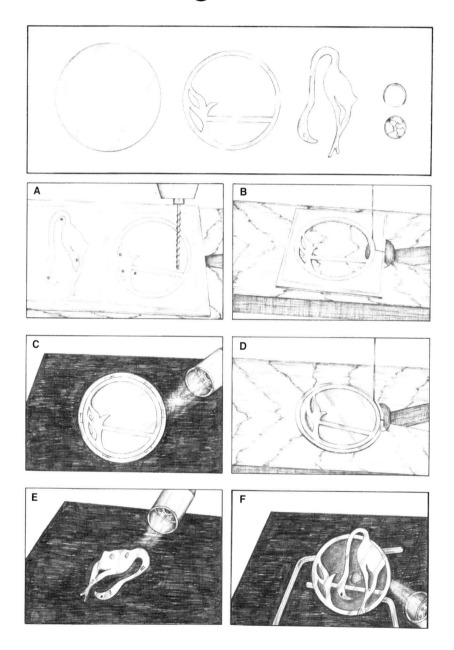

Flamingos were a much beloved motif of the Art Nouveau movement. The graceful indolence of the neck, combined with a certain knowing glint in the eye, somehow came to typify the spirit of an age.

This particular design is based on a famous piece by the German "Jungendstil" artist and historian Josef Hofstetter. Although originally executed in gold and enamel, the design lends itself elegantly to this turquoise-and-silver "shadowbox" treatment. The flamingo's neck can be bent to accommodate different-sized stones if need be.

MATERIALS

(1) Turquoise round (approximately 7mm)
(1) Strip of bezel wire (approximately 1 inch)
(1) Piece 20 gauge sheet silver (approximately 1¾ by 2½ inches)
(1) 1½ inch diameter circle of 22 gauge silver
   Medium and easy solder

TOOLS

Hand drill with ¹/₃₂ inch bit
Jeweler's saw, #1 and #1/0 blade
Propane torch
Large pattern file
Half-round needle file
Curved burnisher and/or stone pusher
Oxidizing solution and fine tip brush
Pumice powder and soft toothbrush

STEPS

1) Transfer the flamingo and the plant-and-horizon background to the piece of 20 gauge sheet, and drill holes where indicated (Box A).
2) Cut out.
3) Pierce out the interior of the design with a #1/0 blade, then cut around the outline until the piece drops free (Box B).
4) Cut a circle 1½ inches in diameter from a piece of 22 gauge sheet silver. Clean the surface, flux it, and lay it on the charcoal block.

5) After the landscape has been refined with the half-round needle file, sand the bottom, flux it and place it on the larger circle. Medium solder is placed around the edge (Box C) to keep it from getting on the background (solder tends to produce a somewhat uneven patina when oxidized). Heat until the solder flows, pickle, and rinse.

6) Saw off the extra edge around the piece (Box D), then file until the seam between the two pieces is no longer visible.

7) Flux the back of the flamingo and premelt easy solder snippets at the places where the flamingo will come in contact with the background (Box E). Pickle, rinse, and sand clean.

8) Make the bezel for the stone, then set it and the flamingo into their respective places in the design to check the fit. If the stone is a little too large, the flamingo's neck can be gently bent towards the left-hand side of the piece to make room.

9) Place bent coat-hanger wires on the charcoal block and lay the constructed backing piece on top of them. Flux and clean all points of contact, place the bezel and the flamingo as shown, and solder them to the main piece using easy solder. Direct the flame under and over the piece to avoid melting the freestanding parts of the flamingo's body (Box F).

10) Solder the findings. There are several possibilities: a wire or sheet "collar" around the neck, a jump ring soldered to the top of the neck, etc. Or the piece can be made into a brooch by soldering brooch findings on the back of the piece.

11) Bezel the stone into the setting. Use the tip of the curved burnisher to get at hard-to-reach places.

12) Buff the piece.

13) After removing all traces of buffing compound, apply oxidizing solution to the background. After it has darkened, rinse the piece in hot water. If you wish, you can create highlights by gently brushing different parts of the background with a soft wet toothbrush dipped in pumice powder.

14) Polish the piece, taking care not to remove the oxidation.

Wire Earrings

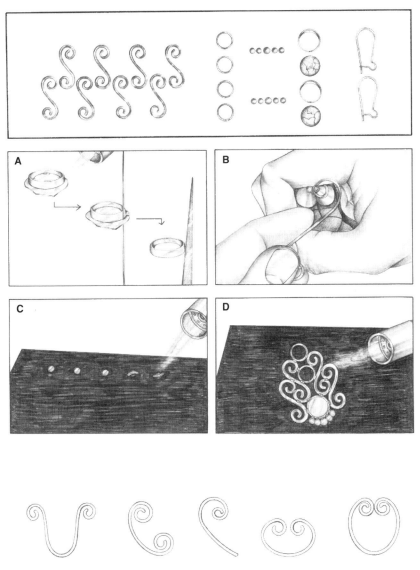

This project serves as an introduction to three important techniques: bending wire scrolls, soldering wire together, and making the little silver spheres which Indian craftsmen call "raindrops." Calibrated turquoise rounds (almost invariably treated) of the size required are available at most jewelry supply shops, often with their own pre-made bezel cups. Providing all junctures between the wires are cleaned and in proper contact, these distinctively Persian-style earrings are much easier to make than their inevitable admirers would suspect.

MATERIALS

(2) small turquoise rounds, 7 to 9 mm
    14 inches 18 gauge round wire
(4) jump rings
(10) "raindrops" made from scrap wire or sheet
(2) wire earring findings
    medium and easy solder

TOOLS

household wire nippers
round-nose pliers
propane torch fitted with fine tip
needle file
curved burnisher and/or stone pusher

STEPS

1) Purchase a ready-made bezel cup or make your own in the manner described in Chapter 12 (Box A).

2) Cut the 18 gauge wire into equal lengths of 1¾ inches with wire nippers, then twist them into double scrolls (Box B).

3) Make a few shallow holes in the edge of the charcoal block using a small screw. Place a piece of scrap silver or wire over or in each of the holes and heat them until they melt (Box C). They will obediently form little spheres in accordance with the laws of surface tension. (Flat-bottomed spheres can be formed on a firebrick.)

4) Make the jump rings and solder the ends together with medium solder.

5) Lightly sand all areas of the design which are to be soldered. Then lay out the design on the block, touch all points of contact lightly with flux-moistened brush, and heat for a moment with the torch. This will adhere the parts together, so that you are not constantly knocking them out of place when you are distributing the solder snippets. Snippets of easy solder should be placed as shown in Box D.

Note: It is important that the surface of the charcoal block where the design is laid out be flat. If not, take an old file and even it off. Many jewelers keep a block of natural restaurant pumice around expressly for wire projects; its surface doesn't become pitted and uneven as rapidly as charcoal.

6) After soldering the piece together, bezel the stones into the bezel cups, buff and polish, then loop the earring findings through the top jump rings.

Once you get the hang of it, you will find that wire patterns offer endless opportunities for improvisation. A few of the most common wire shapes used in jewelry making are illustrated below the boxes.

Fish Pendant

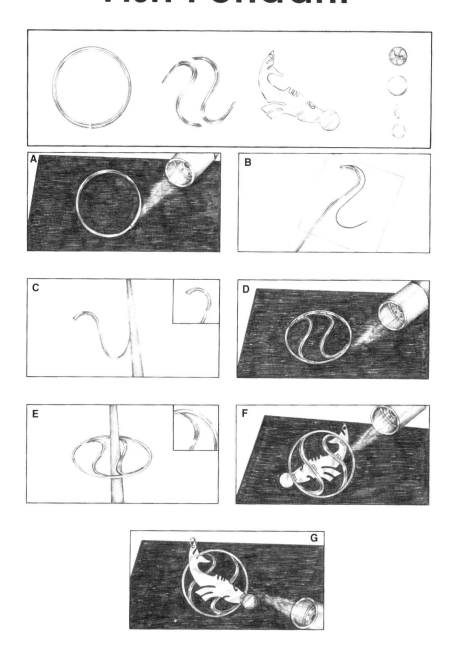

This openwork design was derived from a piece by Edgar Simpson, a leading light of the turn-of-the-century British Art Nouveau movement. Simpson was particularly fond, for reasons unknown, of rendering fish in jewelry and did many outstanding ornaments on the theme. This design is considered one of his masterpieces.

It is a fairly straightforward piece: the fish's features are cut in with a saw and the identical wire "waves" are soldered into the circle. The fish can accommodate different sized and shaped pieces of turquoise by changing the dimensions of the platform near the mouth.

MATERIALS

(1) turquoise round, approximately 7 mm
(1) piece bezel wire, approximately ⅞ inch long
    7½-inch 10 gauge half-round wire
(1) piece 20 gauge sheet, 1⅜ inches square
    1-inch 20 gauge wire (for jump ring and "mouth")
    hard, medium, and easy solder

TOOLS

jeweler's saw with #2 blade
hand drill with ¹/₃₂-inch drill bit
propane torch with fine tip
baseball bat mandrel
rawhide hammer
round-nose pliers
half-round needle file
curved burnisher and/or stone pusher

STEPS

1) Cut the fish according to the pattern in the pattern box by sawing along the cuts with a #2 blade. The holes in the tail and the eye are drilled.

2) Make a ring of 10 gauge wire approximately 1⅛ inches in

diameter from 3¾ inches of annealed wire. The easiest way to do this is to insert the bat through the 1⅛-inch hole in the circle template, mark it off, and wrap wire around it at that spot. Mark and cut the wire, file the edges even, press fit them together, and solder the ring with hard solder (Box A). The solder should be placed *underneath* the juncture—the heat will draw it up through the join.

3) Twist two 1¾-inch lengths of wire into the shape shown in the pattern box, using the round-nose pliers. The simplest way to do this is to first make the initial loop and then slowly bend, referring frequently to the original pattern (Box B). You will find this easier if you anneal the wire first.

4) File the ends of the wire flat, so that they will make a snug fit with the inner edge of the circle (Box C).

5) Test the fit of the wires in the circle, bending and filing as necessary until a good fit is obtained. They are reversed in the design in relation to each other; i.e., the small loop on one is parallel to the large loop on the other.

6) Sand all points of contact clean and place medium solder as shown in Box D. Heat till the solder flows, pickle, and rinse.

7) File the insides of the loop with the half-round needle file (Box E) until they blend with the outer circle (Box E, insert).

8) Position the fish and the wire circle as shown in Box F, place easy solder at the points of contact, and heat till the solder flows, pickle, and rinse.

9) Make the bezel for the stone. Solder the bezel and the jump ring at the same time using easy solder (Box G). File around the edge of the bezel platform to eliminate the visible seam.

10) Bezel in the stone, buff, and polish.

Inlaid Ring

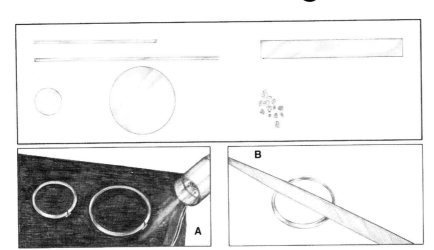

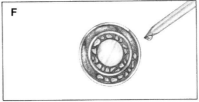

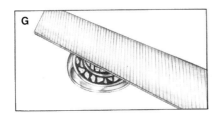

This project introduces a simple method of forming channels for inlay using round wire circles soldered to a base. A simple "bull's-eye" pattern has been used in this case, but more asymmetrical patterns are possible. If you wish, a stone may be mounted in the center circle.

The project is made easier by the predetermined ring sizes, although channels could be any size preferred. Inexpensive turquoise, either cheap Persian or dyed, is crushed up and used for inlay material.

MATERIALS

$4\frac{3}{4}$ inches of 16 gauge wire
(1) $\frac{7}{8}$-inch and (1) $\frac{3}{8}$-inch circle of 18 gauge sheet
(1) strip of 18 or 20 gauge silver for ring shank
    crushed turquoise
    medium and easy solder

TOOLS

jeweler's saw with #1 blade
propane torch with fine tip
ring mandrel
rawhide mallet
garden file (or other inexpensive file)

STEPS

1) Make two rings, one with $\frac{5}{8}$-inch and the other with $\frac{7}{8}$-inch outside diameter (these correspond to $2\frac{1}{2}$ and $9\frac{3}{4}$ on the ring mandrel, and are made from $1\frac{7}{8}$-inch and $2\frac{5}{8}$-inch lengths of wire respectively). Try to get it as exactly as possible, but a little leeway here and there is no catastrophe.

2) Place the press-fitted ends of the rings over fluxed snippets of medium solder and heat until the solder flows up into the seam (Box A). Pickle and rinse.

3) File the bottom of the larger ring flat (Box B). This is done so

that the seam between the outer ring and the outside edge of the circle can be filed away without losing too much of the wire.

4) Cut out the two circles of 18 gauge sheet. After sanding all points of contact clean, set up the wires and circles as shown in Box C and solder the whole construction together with easy solder (Insert shows center circle with a piece of solder on back.)

5) File around the outside edge of the circle until the seam between the wire and the sheet is no longer visible.

6) Measure a shank of the appropriate length and solder it to the back of the circle with easy solder (Box D).

7) Oxidize the channels formed by the wires (Box E).

8) Crush up the turquoise. This can be done by squeezing it in the flat-nose pliers or hammering it in a leather bag, old athletic sock, etc. Then mix up some *slow-drying* two-part epoxy and place it in the inside channel. Using a nail or a matchstick made sticky with the glue, place the turquoise in the channel as closely as possible until it is filled. Then repeat the same procedure with the outside channel (Box F). Don't worry about pieces sticking up; they will be filed down later. However, try to have as few pieces as possible *below* the tops of the rings to avoid a "sunken" look later.

9) Allow the epoxy to dry overnight.

10) File the top of the ring with a fairly coarse garden (lawnmower) file until the stone and epoxy are ground down to the level of the silver (Box G). Bang the file against the side of the work bench periodically to unclog the teeth. Don't use your good files for this part of the job. If you wish to spend a little extra, you can purchase a heatless carborundum wheel for your buffing motor to do the job quite a bit faster. If you go this route, remember to wet it down frequently to avoid overheating the stones. Do not, however, use the cotton buffing wheels—they will gouge out the epoxy much faster than the stone, leaving the surface of the ring with an uneven, bumpy look.

11) Once you have evened out the stones to approximately the level of the silver, continue the finishing job with a scotch stone or facial pumice block (Box H). This will further refine and even out the surface.

12) Continue finishing with finer grades of sandpaper.

13) Finally, give the piece a once-over with tripoli and then rouge. If you are using hand buffing sticks you have nothing to worry about, but remember: be careful when buffing and polishing inlay on the machine!

Inlaid Brooch

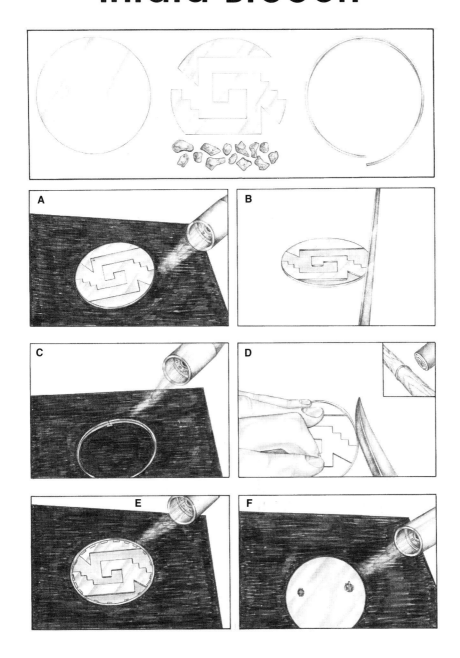

The Yahuitlan Brooch, of which this project is a specially adapted replica, is perhaps the most famous single piece of Mesoamerican jewelry to survive the Spanish Conquest. Now on exhibit at the Museo Nacional de Antropologia of Mexico, it was discovered near Oaxaca in 1903, resting on the chest of an ancient skeleton. The particular power of the symbol comes from the startling figure-ground reversal which, in the light of its frequent appearance on the shields of Montezuma's warriors, was no doubt considered a way of confusing adversaries—or at least bringing on a few Excedrin headaches in the ranks.

In this version of the piece, the most critical step is fashioning a close-fitting outer ring, a task for which our trusty baseball bat mandrel will prove itself admirably suited.

MATERIALS

Approx. 25 medium-sized turquoise chips
(1) 1⅝-inch circle of 22 gauge silver
(1) piece of 18 gauge sheet silver, approx. 1¾ inches square.
5¼ inches of 12 gauge half-round wire
Medium and easy solder
Oxidizing solution and fine-tipped brush

TOOLS

Jeweler's saw with #1 blade
Flat and four-square needle files
Large garden file (or other inexpensive file)
Propane torch, medium tip
Baseball bat mandrel
Rawhide hammer
Curved burnisher

STEPS

1) Cut out a 1⅝-inch circle from a sheet of 22 gauge sheet silver.
2) Cut out the overlay pieces shown in the pattern box from a piece of 18 gauge sheet. Once the pattern is sawed out, the longer

edges can be trued by clamping the piece in a bench vise and giving it a few judicious swipes with the large pattern file. The "stairsteps" and other sharp corners should be refined with flat and four-square needle files.

3) Solder the overlay pieces onto the circle with medium solder (Box A).

4) Carefully file the edge of the piece all the way around, to even off any bumps or places where the overlay protrudes over the edge (Box B). Later this will be essential to making a snug fit with the surrounding ring.

5) Make the surrounding ring from a length of annealed 12 gauge half-round wire. It should have an inside diameter of 1⅝ inches (about 5¼ inches of wire). You can slip the bat mandrel through the 1⅝-inch hole in the circle template and mark it to provide a guide. If you suspect that you no longer *have* a 1⅝-inch circle, measure the ring as you would a stone for a bezel, wrapping the wire tightly around the circle and marking it.

6) File the ends even, press fit them together, and solder the ring together with a snippet of medium solder placed under the juncture of the ends.

7) Fit the ring around the circle, using the curved burnisher to help "bezel" it on. This is done by first fitting part of the wire circle around the piece, then burnishing around it until enough slack is created to allow the rest of the ring to be pushed over the edge of the piece (Box D). Be sure that any "burr" on the edge of the circle which may be left over from previous filing has been eliminated, as this can prevent the ring from slipping on.

If it is just too tight, use a rawhide mallet or, if that doesn't work, a ball peen or chasing hammer, to pound it on the mandrel until it fits (Box D, insert). If it was too big in the first place it will just have to be redone. The object is to get as tight a fit as possible so that the edges of the overlay pattern and the inside of the surrounding ring will form a close, invisible join when soldered.

8) Once you have obtained a good fit, place a generous number of easy solder snippets on the edge between the main piece and the surrounding ring and heat until the solder flows (Box E).

9) Solder the brooch findings on the back of the piece, using easy solder. The solder can either be placed around the findings or premelted in place (Box F).

10) Follow a procedure for inlaying the stone similar to Project 9 (Inlaid Ring) first oxidizing the background and then using epoxy to set the stones. In this case, getting the fragments to fit closely is a little more critical to the success of the design. Try to use larger chips, putting them together like a jigsaw puzzle.

11) Finishing also follows a procedure similar to the Inlaid Ring. The facial pumice stone is much more useful than the scotch stone with this piece, as it will cover more surface area.

Flower Bracelet

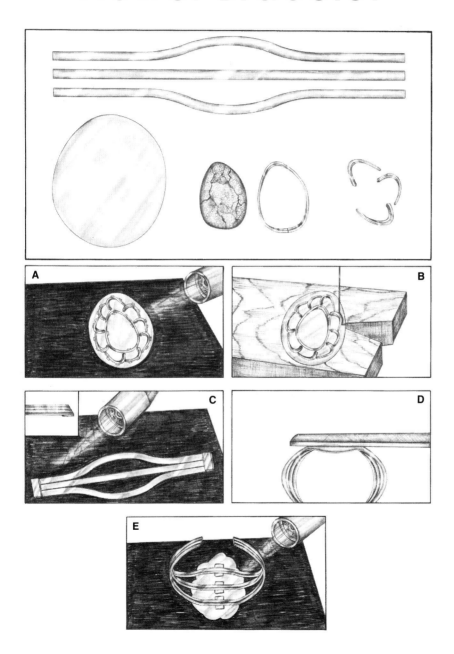

Navajo medicine men are renowned for their unique (and often surprisingly efficacious) methods of healing. One frequently used ceremony, consisting of delicately balancing chips of turquoise on the petals of a freshly-bloomed flower, inspired this particular piece. The silver wire petals against the dark black oxidation is a striking way to set off the blue of the stone.

MATERIALS

(1) turquoise cab (any shape); bezel wire to fit
12 gauge, half-round wire
15 to 18 inches 8 gauge, half-round wire
18 gauge silver sheet
Hard, medium, and easy solder

TOOLS

Jeweler's saw with #1 blade
Round-nose pliers
Wire snips
Cleanburn or Mapp gas, large torch tip
Needle files
Large pattern file
Bracelet mandrel (optional)
Curved burnisher and/or stone pusher

STEPS

1) Bend lengths of 12 gauge half-round wire into loops using the round-nose pliers. The bend is made by working the pliers gradually around the wire.

2) Make the bezel (soldering it with hard solder), sand the bottom, and true it.

3) Cut out a piece of 18 gauge sheet silver slightly bigger than the size of the "flower." Sand the bottoms of the wires and the surface of the sheet.

4) Flux the bottom plate, set the bezel in place and allow to dry

(this way the bezel will not get knocked out of place when you are placing the wires). Arrange the wires around the bezel and place medium solder in the bezel and around the edges of the wire (Box A).

5) Heat the piece until the solder flows; pickle and rinse.

6) Saw around the outlines of the "petals" (Box B), then file the edges smooth. It will not be possible to eliminate the seam without filing away a lot of wire, but the double-layered look, in this case, is an attractive addition to the piece.

7) Measure the wrist, and cut the 8 gauge half-round wires to the proper size. After annealing, bend them to the shapes shown in the pattern box. This is done by first making the middle kink and then bending up the ends. A suggested method: stick the ring mandrel through the center hold in the bench pin, and make the center bend around that. Then, holding the wire in the middle, bend up the ends on the edge of the work table.

8) Lay the wires on the charcoal block, cut two strips ⅜ by ¼ inch from the 18 gauge sheet, then solder them to the ends of the wires with medium solder (Box C). It will be helpful to use a hotter burning gas (Mapp or Cleanburn) in this step and the steps that follow due to the size of the pieces being heated.

9) Bevel the inside edges of the strips with a half-round needle file so that they will not scratch the wrist when the bracelet is worn.

10) Bend the bracelet into shape using your hands, if they are strong enough, or the homemade bracelet mandrel and a rawhide mallet (see Chapter 13). Then file the top flat with a large pattern file (Box D) and sand it smooth in preparation for soldering.

11) Place snippets of easy solder as shown in Box E, and solder the bracelet shank to the platform. After waiting a minute, quench the piece in *hot* pickle to minimize the chance of cracking from the change in temperature.

12) Buff the bracelet (don't forget the inside of the shank). Be very careful if you are using a polishing motor; the ends of the bracelet are particularly prone to getting caught by the wheel.

13) Oxidize the flower's petals.

14) Bezel in the stone and polish the piece.

Elk Bolo Tie

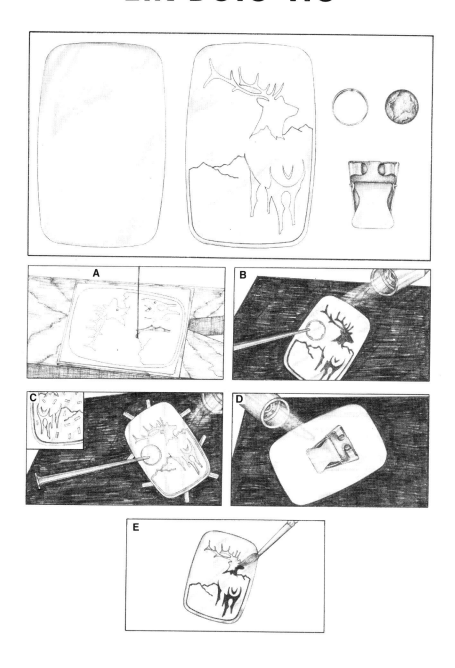

This scene of a bull elk surveying his wintry domain lends itself well to Hopi-style overlay techniques. Give this one to your favorite Jack London fan.

You will definitely need Cleanburn or Mapp gas to heat this piece as it is relatively large and heavy. Also, it is recommended that you use a nail as a "heat-sink" since the bezel can melt under the heat required to get the bolo up to soldering temperature.

MATERIALS

(1) turquoise round between 10 mm and 15 mm.
   Bezel wire
(1) 3¼ by 2¼-inch piece of 18 gauge sheet silver
(1) 3¼ by 2¼-inch piece of 20 gauge sheet silver
   Commercial bolo tie findings
   Hard, medium, and easy solder

TOOLS

Jeweler's saw, #1 and #1/0 blade
Hand drill with ¹/₃₂-inch drill bit
Cleanburn or Mapp gas torch tip
Bent coat-hanger wires
Nail or coat-hanger wire for "heat-sink"
Oxidizing solution and fine-tip brush
Curved burnisher and/or stone pusher

STEPS

1) Glue the design to the 18 gauge sheet and drill holes where shown. Then pierce out the design as follows: for the basic shape of the elk (head, legs and tail) use a #1/0 saw blade to carefully cut the design. For the mountains and the border, use the #1 saw blade (Box A).

2) Make a bezel for the stone. Flux the top piece, set the bezel in position, and allow the flux to adhere it in place. Then place medium

solder, set the nail on the bezel, and heat until the solder flows (Box B). Pickle and rinse.

3) Cut out the base from the 20 gauge silver sheet, and set it down on coat-hanger wires. Place medium solder on the back of the cut-out overlay as shown in Box C (insert). In placing solder, the idea is to steer clear of the lines so that the solder doesn't flow onto the parts of the base piece which will later be oxidized. In addition, the solder should be far enough away from the "mountains" and the outline so that it will not accidently fill in the cut lines.

4) Place the nail as a "heat-sink," and direct the flame of the torch over and under the piece until the solder flows (Box C), pickle and rinse.

5) Solder on the bolo tie finding using easy solder (Box D).

6) Bezel in the stone and buff the piece.

7) Brush in the oxidation (Box E), then gently polish the piece.

Turquoise Maiden Buckle

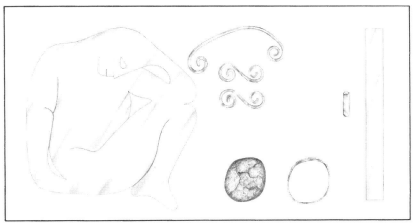

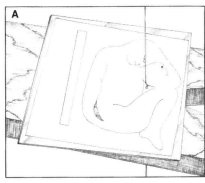

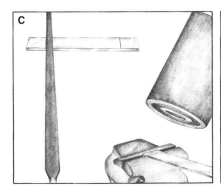

An old astrological text recommends that "on Friday, the day of Venus, one should wear a turquoise set in the design of a king on a camel or a naked maiden." We chose the latter. You can wear this pensive wire-coiffed lady any day of the week. The design, when reduced, also makes a lovely brooch.

MATERIALS

(1) medium size turquoise cab (any shape)
Bezel wire
3-inch by 3-inch sheet of 16 gauge silver
7-inch 18 gauge wire
¼-inch 16 gauge wire
Easy solder

TOOLS

Hand-drill with ³/₆₄-inch drill bit
Jeweler's saw with #4 blade
Round-nose pliers
Bent coat-hanger wire
Triangular or knife-edge needle file
Mapp gas or Clean-Burn, medium torch tip
Bench vise
Rawhide hammer
Curved burnisher and/or stone pusher

STEPS

1) Saw along the lines of the pattern in the pattern box with the heavy saw blade, piercing out the inside lines first. From the left-over silver, cut a strip ¼ by 2⅞ inches for a buckle hitch (Box A).

2) Cut the wire into (1) 3¼-inch and (2) 1¾-inch lengths. Bend them with the round-nose pliers according to the pattern or make up your own.

3) Make the bezel for the stone.

4) Place the piece on coat-hanger wires as shown. (This will help you avoid melting the wires or bezel while bringing the larger piece up to soldering temperature). Place easy solder as shown and heat the piece until it flows (Box B). Allow the piece to cool to just below dull red, then quench in *hot* pickle.

5) File away the seam between the sheet and the bezel.

6) After filing grooves with the triangular or knife-edge needle file, bend the buckle hitch as shown in Box C. The bend is made ¼ inch from the end of the strip. Also, cut the little peg of 16 gauge wire.

7) Solder the buckle hitch and peg onto the back with easy solder (Box D). The buckle is thick enough that this should not affect previously soldered joins. The hitch will stand unsupported; the peg is held in position with the locking tweezers or ''third hand'' while it is being soldered. Allow to cool slightly then quench in *hot* pickle.

8) Finish the piece before bezeling the stone. If the firestain is excessive, you can 1) bright dip the piece to build up a layer of fine silver and then polish lightly; 2) buff off the firestain completely; or 3) buff it off selectively, trying to incorporate it into the design—the color can add interest to the piece.

9) Hand-bend the buckle into a slight curve so it will better conform to the waist when worn.

Hopi Indian Buckle

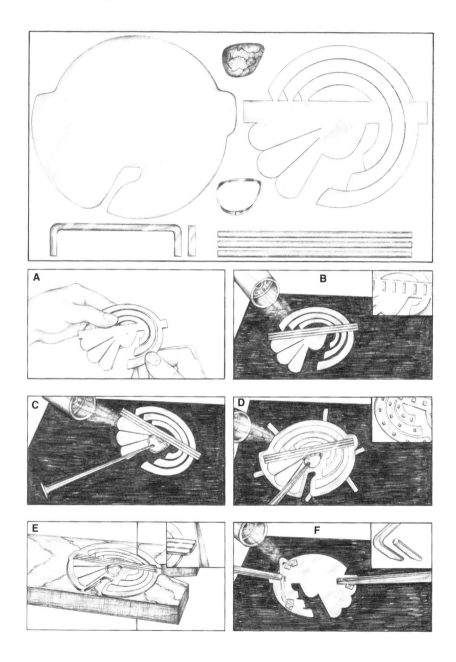

This unique buckle is based on a pin made by the great Hopi artist, Travis Yaiva, in the 1940s. Yaiva's piece is one of the Indian silver masterworks in the Museum of Northern Arizona.

The main trick with this one is getting everything, i.e., the half-round wires and the top piece, to lay flat enough to be soldered. Just be patient. Careful bending will pay off in spades when it's time to solder.

MATERIALS

(1) medium turquoise cab, any shape
Bezel wire
(1) 3-by-6-inch piece of 20 gauge silver sheet
8¼ inches of 12 gauge half-round wire
2½ inches of 10 gauge round wire
Hard, medium, and easy solder

TOOLS

Jeweler's saw with #2 saw blade
Cleanburn or Mapp gas, medium torch tip
Nail or coat-hanger wire for "heat-sink"
Bent coat-hanger wires
Large pattern file
Needle files
Flat-nose pliers
Locking tweezers
Oxidizing solution and fine-tip brush
Curved burnisher and/or stone pusher

STEPS

1) Cut the patterns shown in the pattern box from the piece of 20 gauge sheet silver. The section where the bezel will be placed should be shaped to the stone you will use. Be particularly careful cutting in the lines of the semicircles in the top piece, as you will not be able to make corrections by filing.

2) After you have sawed it out, gently bend the "arms" of the design out just a little to enlarge the space between them (Box A).

3) Cut the 12 gauge, half-round wire into even 2¾-inch lengths. Bend them until they lie flat on the table and are parallel to one another. Place medium solder snippets as shown, and heat until the solder flows (Box B). The wires will "sink" a little with heat. Keep your pointed tool handy to *gently* push them down in places where they are not in sufficient contact with the main piece to allow the solder to flow. Quench the piece in *hot* pickle and rinse.

4) Flux the area where the bezel will go, set the bezel down, and allow the flux to dry. Then place the nail as a "heat-sink" and solder with medium solder (Box C). Quench in *hot* pickle and rinse.

5) Place the base piece on bent coat-hanger wires, and flux it thoroughly. After making sure that the top piece will lie flat, place snippets of easy solder on the back of it, as shown. Then place the top piece into position, and again using the nail as a "heat-sink," heat the entire piece until the solder flows (Box D). Wait a minute or two, quench in *hot* pickle, and rinse.

6) Cut around the outline of the design but only part-way into the "petals" which radiate from the bezel (Box E). *DO NOT* cut into the semicircular "arms."

7) File around the edge of the piece with large pattern file and needle files until the seam between the top and bottom pieces disappears. Also, round off the corners of the wires (Box E, insert).

8) Bend 2¼ inches of 10 gauge round wire a quarter inch from each end using the flat-nose pliers or the bench vise and a rawhide hammer (see Project 13). Bevel the bottoms of the buckle hitch and the left-over ¼-inch peg as shown (Box F, insert). Flux the back of the piece, elevate the locking tweezers in such a way that they hold the hitch and peg in place (you can use a "third hand" for this) and solder them on with easy solder. The findings can be soldered on one at a time if you only have one pair of tweezers. Quench in hot pickle and rinse.

9) Bezel the stone, and buff the piece.

10) Oxidize the lines and polish the entire piece.

Glossary

ALLOY: A combination of two or more metals, usually done to create greater strength and durability.

ANNEALING: The process of heating metal to red-hot temperature and then cooling it with the purpose of rendering it more pliable for working.

BACKING: A material applied to the back of a piece of turquoise to reinforce the stone. Sometimes composed of epoxy but more often of "liquid bronze" compound, it is considered an ethical practice as long as it is not used solely to stretch the weight of a stone.

BAROQUE: An irregularly-shaped cut stone. American turquoise is almost always cut in baroque forms to minimize waste.

BENCH PIN: A wooden wedge or slat with a V-notch cut in the end. It is attached to the workbench and used to support work while it is being filed or sawn.

BEVEL: An angled edge on a stone or a piece of silver.

BEZEL: A thin surrounding strip of metal which is pushed up around a stone to hold it in place. Bezels of fine (q.v.) silver are the most frequently used settings for turquoise cabs.

BUFFING: In general, refers to refinishing a piece of jewelry by rubbing it, either mechanically or by hand, with a polishing compound. More specifically, refers to using abrasives such as tripoli (q.v.) to smooth the metal surface before final polishing.

BURNISHER: A smooth steel tool used to press a bezel tightly against a stone.

CARAT: Standard unit weight used in the gem trade. The original carat was the equivalent of a carob seed, historically favored by Eastern pearl traders as a unit of measurement because of its remarkably uniform weight (approximately .197 grams). The modern metric carat is equal to one-fifth of a gram.

CABOCHON: A stone with a smooth curved surface (from the French for "like a bald head").

CHALK: In the turquoise trade, a soft or porous grade of stone which must be treated before it can be used as a gemstone.

CHRYSOCOLLA: A blue copper mineral often mistaken for genuine turquoise.

CLEANBURN, MAPP GAS: A new high-temperature canister gas which burns 800 degrees hotter than propane.

CROCUS CLOTH: Paper impregnated with red iron oxide and used in fine finishing work.

DOP STICK: A wooden dowel to which a stone is attached with dopping wax for final grinding and polishing. "Dop" is an old Dutch word for "shell," referring to the shape of stone-holders used in former times by diamond cutters.

EMERY PAPER: An abrasive sheet coated with powdered emery (an inexpensive variety of corundum), garnet, or carborundum and used for smoothing and refining metal surfaces.

FINDINGS: The various catches, clasps, and fittings, homemade or commercially manufactured, used to fasten jewelry to the body.

FINE: A term denoting purity in a precious metal, i.e., a metal which has not been alloyed (q.v.) with another substance.

FIRESCALE (FIRESTAIN, FIRECOAT): A discoloring coat of copper oxide which forms on precious metal alloys during the heating process.

FLUX: A substance used to encourage the flow of solder. Flux keeps air from coming into contact with the surface of the heated metal, thus preventing the formation of surface oxides.

FORGING: The process of hammering metal on a hard surface in order to flatten, stretch, or otherwise alter its form.

FREE FORM: See Baroque.

INLAY: A technique of embedding a decorative material in another substance in such a way that they form a level surface. Craftsmen from the ancient Egyptians to the modern Zuñi Indians have used this method with turquoise to great effect.

JOIN: The juncture at which two pieces of metal are soldered together.

JUMP RING: A small circle of wire generally used to suspend a piece of jewelry from a chain or neck ring, or to hang one element of the piece from the main body of the work.

MANDREL: A graduated steel or hardwood form over which metal is shaped.

MANIPULATED: Natural turquoise which has undergone some form of man-made treatment or alteration.

MATRIX: Inclusions of other unrelated substances in a stone. In the case of turquoise, these may be clays, limestone, pyrite, or quartz. In the past, the presence of matrix adversely affected the value of a stone, but today a turquoise with good matrix commands the highest market price.

NEEDLE FILES: Small, generally fine cut files used in jewelry finishing work.

OVERLAY: A style of jewelry in which the design is formed by a cut-out pattern soldered to a backing plate. In Hopi-style overlay, the recessed parts of the pattern are first textured and then blackened by oxidation (q.v.).

OXIDATION: 1. The deliberate coloring of precious metals with a chemical agent. 2. A patina which forms on precious metal alloys due to a reaction with air.

PAILLON, PALLET: See Snippet.

PATTERN FILE: Generally, a large file used in jewelry work to remove large amounts of metal.

PATINA: The surface appearance of metal resulting from natural aging or specific chemical treatment.

PERSIAN: Turquoise from what is now modern Iran. The best grade is an almost translucent "robin's egg" blue and takes a very high polish.

PICKLE: An acid solution used to remove surface oxides from metal, usually immediately after heating or soldering.

PIERCING: The process whereby an interior design is sawed out of a sheet of metal.

PLASTICIZING: The injection of turquoise with a clear or tinted plastic in order to fill in pores so that the stone can accept a polish or to deepen or stabilize the color. The treatment is generally permanent.

PLATFORM: That part of a ring which sits on top of the finger.

PLATE SHEARS: Metal-cutting scissors used on solder and lighter gauges of precious metal.

PUMICE: A volcanic rock used in powdered form as a polishing agent.

QUENCH: To rapidly cool a piece of hot metal, usually by immersion in a liquid.

RAINDROP: A small silver sphere made by heating a piece of scrap silver to its melting point. Used for decorative purposes.

RECONSTITUTED: Refers to stones moulded from a mixture of finely-ground turquoise chips and epoxy.

RIFFLER FILE (DIE-SINKER'S FILE): A file with curved ends used for getting into hard to reach places when finishing in a piece of metal work.

RING MANDREL: A tapered, solid steel cylinder used for forming and measuring rings.

RING SIZER: A collection of graduated metal or plastic rings strung on a hoop, each one corresponding to a standard ring size.

ROUGE: A waxy polishing compound usually containing red iron oxide, used to give a final mirror-like polish to gold or silver.

SANDCASTING: A technique, pioneered by American Indian craftsmen, for casting individual pieces of jewelry. A form is carved out of a piece of tufa stone or pumice, then filled with molten metal.

SCOTCH STONE: A grey, slate-like stone used wet in jewelry finishing work. Also called Water of Ayr stone or Tam O'Shanter stone.

SEAFOAM: A turquoise nugget with a frothy-looking surface texture.

SEAM: In soldering, the soldered edge between two pieces of metal. In mining, a vein of mineral.

SHADOWBOX: A popular Navajo construction style in which a stone is set on an oxidized base plate surrounded by a polished overlay border, creating a recessed effect.

SHANK: The part of a ring which encircles the finger.

SNIPPET: A small piece of solder.

SOLDER: A low-melting alloy used to join metal. Silver solder is referred to as "hard" solder, as opposed to lower melting lead-based "soft" solders.

SPAREX: A mild acid compound used to remove surface discolorations resulting from heating and soldering.

SPIDERWEB (SPIDER WEBB): The fine, web-like matrix (q.v.) pattern which appears in some turquoise stones. A well-distributed network of black lines in a dense blue stone is highly prized in today's turquoise market.

SPLIT SHANK: A shank whose ends, rather than being joined together, are soldered separately to the platform of the ring.

STABILIZED: The process of stabilization is used with porous stones of good color to keep them from fading with wear. The pores are sealed by injecting the stone with a sodium silica gel or plastic polymer, which hardens the stone and makes it impervious to body oils and chemicals.

STERLING: Silver which is 92.5 percent pure, the remaining proportion consisting of copper. Nearly all silver used in jewelry work is sterling.

SWEAT SOLDERING: A technique of melting solder between two metal surfaces in order to join them.

SYNTHETIC: Artificial turquoise consisting of a man-made compound with the same chemical make-up as natural turquoise. Often a synthetic matrix is added. These drab, dark-blue stones are rarely mistaken for the genuine article.

THIRD HAND: A stand fitted with locking tweezers or alligator clips, used to hold jewelry work in position during soldering operations.

TREATED: Low grade turquoise whose appearance has been improved by filling the pores with wax, paraffin, mineral oil, plastic or other color-enhancing substances.

TRIPOLI: A finely-grained silica buffing compound used to smooth the surface of a jewelry piece prior to final polishing.

TRUMMING (THRUMMING): Polishing difficult to reach parts in a piece of metalwork using a string which has been charged with abrasive.

VARISCITE: Like turquoise, variscite is a hydrous aluminum phosphate. Usually lustrous green in color, the stone is often mistaken for green varieties of turquoise such as "Pixie" or "Sadie Green."

YELLOW OCHRE: A powdered earth mineral used to prevent the flow of solder.

ZAM (ZAM CROCUS): A commercial polishing compound, normally used on chrome or steel, which has gained widespread popularity among craftsmen working in turquoise and silver.

ZAT: "A good stone, in short, must possess an indefinable property called 'Zat' which is something like the water of diamond or the lustre of a pearl. A fine colored turquoise without the 'Zat' is not worth much." (From *The Turquoise* by Joseph Pogue.)

Bibliography

JEWELRY MAKING

Morton, Philip. *Contemporary Jewelry.* New York: Holt, Rinehart, and Winston, 1976. A very good survey of historical and contemporary art history combined with an up-to-date jewelry text.

Choate, Sharr. *Creative Gold- and Silversmithing.* New York: Crown, 1970. A thoroughly illustrated manual and reference work for intermediate craftsmen.

Von Neumann, Robert. *The Design and Creation of Jewelry.* Philadelphia: Chilton Book Company, 1972. A clear, straightforward exposition of jewelry making from simple to advanced methods. The best book of its kind on the subject.

Branson, Oscar T. *Indian Jewelry Making.* Tucson: Treasure Chest Publications, Inc., 1977. Manages to cover all the essentials in 60 pages of well-chosen photographs, accompanied by a minimum of text.

Hunt, Ben W. *Indian Silversmithing.* New York: Macmillan Publishing Co., Inc., 1960. A perennial practical how-to book on the subject of traditional Native American techniques.

Rose, Augustus F. and Cirino, Antonio. *Jewelry Making and Design.* New York: Dover, 1967. In this classic, first published in 1918, the authors combine text, photographs, illustrations and projects in a thorough overview of the major constructed jewelry-making techniques.

Murray, Bovin. *Jewelry Making for Schools, Tradesmen, and Craftsmen.* Forest Hills, New York: Bovin Publishing, 1976. A no-nonsense shop manual covering most of the important methods.

Maryon, Herbert. *Metalwork and Enameling.* New York: Dover, 1971. A far-reaching, if under-illustrated, survey of metal techniques by the man who reconstructed the fabulous Sutton Hoo treasure for the British Museum.

Untracht, Oppi. *Metal Techniques for Craftsmen.* New York: Doubleday, 1968. Heavy on info, light on instruction, this is still *the* complete reference work for metal craftsmen.

TURQUOISE

International Turquoise Annual. Reno: Impart Corporation, 1975, 1976.

Pogue, Joseph E. *The Turquoise; a Study of its History, Mineralogy, Geology, Ethnology, Archaeology, Mythology, Folklore, and Technology.* Glorietta, New Mexico: Rio Grande Press, 1972.

Turquoise, Assignment 15 of lesson series, "Colored Stones: Identification, Production, Marketing, Buying, Appraising." Los Angeles: Gemological Institute of America, 1975.

Northrop, Stuart A., Neumann, David L. and Snow, David H. *Turquoise* reprinted from *El Palacio,* vol. 79, no. 1. Santa Fe: Museum of New Mexico Press, 1973.

Bennet, Edna Mae. *Turquoise and the Indian.* Chicago: Sage Books, the Swallow Press, 1970.

Turquoise Blue Book and the Indian Jewelry Digest. Phoenix: Arizona Highways, 1975.

Branson, Oscar T. *Turquoise, the Gem of the Centuries.* Santa Fe: Treasure Chest Publications, Inc., 1975.

Conroy, Kathleen. *What You Should Know About Authentic Indian Jewelry.* Denver: The Gro-Pub Group, 1975.

Suppliers

PRECIOUS METALS

General Refineries
292 Walnut Street
St. Paul, Minn. 55102

Paul H. Gesswein & Co., Inc.
235 Park Avenue South
New York, N.Y. 10003

Grieger's, Inc.
900 S. Arroyo Parkway
Pasadena, Calif. 91109

Handy and Harman
1900 Estes
Elk Grove Village, Ill. 60007

Hauser and Miller Co.
4011 Forest Park Boulevard
St. Louis, Mo. 63108

Swest, Inc.
10803 Composite Drive
(or P.O. Box 2010)
Dallas, Tex. 75220

TOOLS

Allcraft Tool and Supply Co., Inc.
100 Frank Road
Hicksville, N.Y. 11801

William Dixon Co.
750 Washington Avenue
Carlstadt, N. J. 07072

Paul H. Gesswein & Co., Inc.
235 Park Avenue South
New York, N.Y. 10003

Grieger's Inc.
900 South Arroyo Parkway
Pasadena, Calif. 91109

Metal Crafts and Supply Co.
10 Thomas Street
Providence, R.I. 02903

Swest, Inc.
10803 Composite Drive
(or P.O. Box 2010)
Dallas, Tex. 75220

LAPIDARY EQUIPMENT

Grieger's, Inc.
900 South Arroyo Parkway
Pasadena, Calif. 91109

Metal Crafts and Supply Co.
10 Thomas Street
Providence, R.I. 02903

Swest, Inc.
10803 Composite Drive
(or P.O. Box 2010)
Dallas, Tex. 75220

Waldree Lapidary Shop
2267 N. Dearborn Street
Indianapolis, Ind. 46218

TURQUOISE

Argent Express
Highway 88
Pioneer, California 95666

Aurora Chow & Co.
P. O. Box 662
General Post Office
Hong Kong, China

H. H. Benedict & Sons
62 West 47th Street
New York, New York 10036

Colby Mining Corporation
16224 Kivett Lane
Reno, Nevada 89502
and
P. O. Box 344
Steamboat, Nevada 89436

Pierre Gilson SA Lapidaries
Campagne-lez-Wardrecques
62120 AIRE
France

Hamilton Turquoise Company
P. O. Box 2721
Flagstaff, Arizona 86001

J & B Stones
108 Morningside, N.E.
Albuquerque, New Mexico 87108

Ken's
Route 1, Box 1703
Meadow Vista, California 95722

Lapcraft Company
485 Schrock Road
Columbus, Ohio 43229

Om-Shalom Trading Corporation
3298 Mary Street
Coconut Grove, Florida 33133

Raymond Price
P. O. Box 140
St. Michaels, Arizona 86511

Rings 'N Things
1801 Sheridan Boulevard, No. 55
Edgewater, Colorado 80214

Silver Bell Turquoise Company
4295 Stockton Hill Road
Kingman, Arizona 86401

Silver-Gem Trading Co.
4821 45th Street
Lubbock, Texas 79414

Taos East Turquoise Co., Inc.
4600 West 111th (College Blvd.)
Shawnee Mission, Kansas 66207

The Turquoise Mine
Suite 224
12490 N.E. 7th Avenue
North Miami, Florida 33161

Vanguard Abrasive Division
Federal-Mogul Corporation
Lent Avenue
LeRoy, New York 14482

Measurements, Weights, and Solutions

FRACTIONAL AND DECIMAL INCHES TO MILLIMETERS

Fractions	Decimal Inches	Millimeters
1/64	0.0156	0.3969
1/32	0.0313	0.7937
3/64	0.0469	1.1906
1/16	0.0625	1.5875
5/64	0.0781	1.9843
3/32	0.0937	2.3812
7/64	0.1094	2.7781
1/8	0.1250	3.1750
9/64	0.1406	3.5718
5/32	0.1562	3.9687
11/64	0.1719	4.3656
3/16	0.1875	4.7624
13/64	0.2031	5.1593
7/32	0.2187	5.5562
15/64	0.2344	5.9530
1/4	0.2500	6.3499
17/64	0.2656	6.7468
9/32	0.2812	7.1437
19/64	0.2969	7.5405
5/16	0.3125	7.9374
21/64	0.3281	8.3343
11/32	0.3438	8.7312
23/64	0.3594	9.1280
3/8	0.3750	9.5249
25/64	0.3906	9.9217
13/32	0.4062	10.3186
27/64	0.4219	10.7155
7/16	0.4375	11.1124
29/64	0.4531	11.5092
15/32	0.4687	11.9061
31/64	0.4844	12.3030
1/2	0.5000	12.6999

COATED ABRASIVE AND GRIT SIZES

Garnet, Aluminum Oxide, or Silicon Carbide (Carborundum)		Emery
600, 500	—	
400	10/0	
360	—	
320	9/0	
280	8/0	
240	7/0	
220	6/0	
180	5/0	3/0
150	4/0	2/0
120	3/0	—
—	—	0
100	2/0	—
—	—	1/2
80	0	1
—	—	1-1/2
60	1/2	—
—	—	2
50	1	—
—	—	2-1/2
40	1-1/2	—
36	2	—
—	—	3
30	2-1/2	—
24	3	—
20	3-1/2	
16	4	
12	4-1/2	

U. S. STANDARD RING SIZES, LENGTH AND DIAMETER IN INCHES

Size	Length	Diameter	Size	Length	Diameter	Size	Length	Diameter
0	1.429	.458	4	1.835	.586	9	2.35	.746
1/4		.466	4½		.602	9½		.762
1/2		.474	5	1.943	.618	10	2.46	.778
3/4		.482	5½		.634	10½		.794
1	1.528	.490	6	2.045	.650	11	2.56	.810
1½		.506	6½		.666	11½		.826
2	1.632	.522	7	2.15	.682	12	2.63	.842
2½		.538	7½		.698	12½		.858
3	1.735	.554	8	2.25	.714	13	2.76	.874
3½		.570	8½		.730	13½		.890

CIRCUMFERENCE

Diameter (Inches)	Circumference (Inches)	Diameter (Inches)	Circumference (Inches)
3	9³⁄₈	8	25¹⁄₈
3½	10⁵⁄₁₆	8½	26¹¹⁄₁₆
4	12⁹⁄₁₆	9	28¹⁄₄
4½	14¹⁄₈	9½	29¹³⁄₁₆
5	15¹¹⁄₁₆	10	31³⁄₈
5½	17¹⁄₄	10½	32¹⁵⁄₁₆
6	18¹³⁄₁₆	11	34½
6½	20³⁄₈	11½	36¹⁄₈
7	21¹⁵⁄₁₆	12	37¹¹⁄₁₆
7½	23½		

COLORING SOLUTIONS

Applied to silver

Grey: small quantity platinum chloride in alcohol

Dark grey: household bleach

Black: 20g liver of sulphur, 20g ammonia, 1l water, lampblack and beeswax rubbed into deep grooves

Steel blue: heat with chunks of sulphur in a covered can (*caution: toxic fumes require ventilation*)

Reddish-brown: cold solution of 150g barium sulphide in 300ml of water

Gold color: cold solution of 1 g barium sulphide in 200ml of water, or warm solution of 1g ammonium sulphide in 200ml of water

Green color: 1 part iodine, 3 parts hydrochloric acid, 1 part water

Varied colors: 25g liver of sulphur, 10g bicarbonate of soda. 1l of water. Apply under hot running water.

WEIGHTS

Troy Weight

Used in weighing the precious metals.

24 grains = 1 pennyweight (dwt.)
20 dwt. = 1 ounce troy
12 ounces = 1 pound troy
5,760 grains = 1 pound troy

Avoirdupois Weight

Used in weighing base metals.

16 drams (or drachms) = 1 ounce Avoir.
16 ounces = 1 pound Avoir.
16 ounces = 7,000 grains
28 pounds = 1 quarter
4 quarters = 1 hundredweight (cwt.)
20 hundredweight = 1 ton Avoir.

To convert ounces troy to ounces avoirdupois, multiply by 1.09714.
To convert ounces avoirdupois to ounces troy, multiply by 0.91146.

Gram Weight

1 gram = 15.43 grains troy
1.555 grams = 1 pennyweight (dwt.)
31.104 grams = 1 ounce troy
28.35 grams = 1 ounce Avoir.

Carat Weight

Used in weighing precious and semiprecious stones. (The term *Karat* refers to the quality of purity in gold.)

1 carat = $3^1/_{16}$ grains troy
1 carat = .007 ounce Avoir.
1 carat = $^1/_5$ gram

The carat is further divided into *points* for simple measurement:

1 carat = 100 points
$^1/_2$ carat = $^{50}/_{100}$ points
$^1/_4$ carat = $^{25}/_{100}$ points
$^1/_8$ carat = $12^1/_2/100$ points

MILLIMETER STONE SIZES

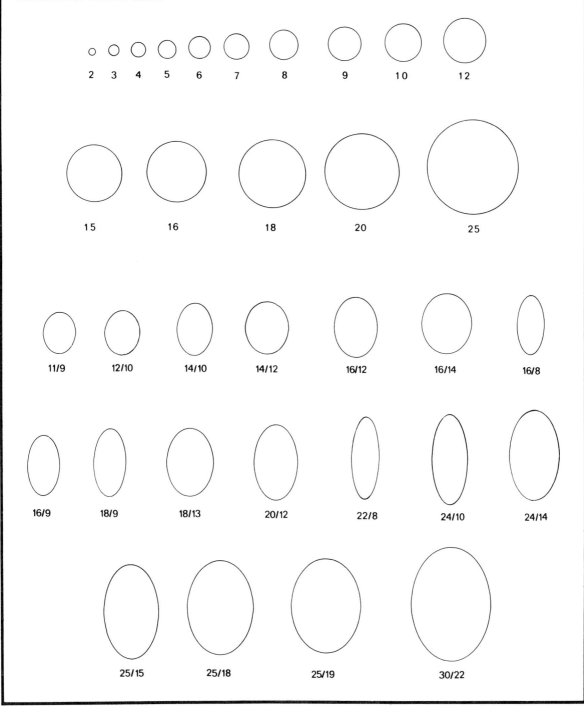

Sterling Silver Specifications

SHEET SILVER

GAUGE		$\frac{1}{1000}''$	WEIGHT 1"x 16"	WEIGHT 6"x 36"
14		.064	2.10	75.6
16		.051	1.65	60.3
18		.040	1.35	48.6
20		.032	1.00	38.6
22		.025	.85	29.4
24		.020	.65	23.4
26		.016	.50	18.6
28		.013	.40	14.6
30		.010	.35	12.1

ROUND WIRE

GAUGE		$\frac{1}{1000}''$	LENGTH per OZ.	OZ. per FOOT
4		.204	5"	2.140
6		.162	9"	1.350
8		.128	15"	.852
10		.102	24"	.536
12		.081	36"	.337
14		.064	5'	.212
16		.051	7'6"	.133
18		.040	12'	.084
20		.032	19'	.053
22		.025	30'	.033

HALF-ROUND WIRE

GAUGE		$\frac{1}{1000}''$	LENGTH per OZ.	OZ. per FOOT
2		.257	8"	1.650
4		.204	13"	1.110
6		.162	18"	.680
8		.128	28"	.424
9		.114	32"	.313
10		.102	42"	.250
12		.081	6'	.170
13		.072	7'	.145
14		.064	9'6"	.120
16		.051	15'	.065

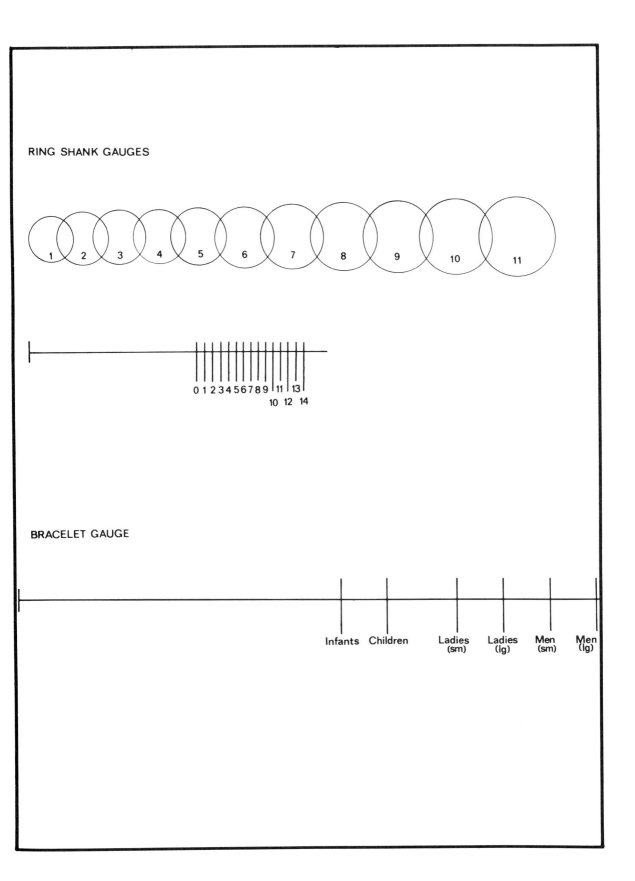

RING SHANK GAUGES

1 2 3 4 5 6 7 8 9 10 11

0 1 2 3 4 5 6 7 8 9 11 13
10 12 14

BRACELET GAUGE

Infants Children Ladies Ladies Men Men
(sm)   (lg)   (sm)   (lg)

Index